The English Project

Stage One
Other Worlds
Edited by Donald Ball

Things Working
Edited by Penny Blackie

Family and School
Edited by David Jackson

Ventures
Edited by Elwyn Rowlands

I Took my Mind a Walk
Edited by George Sanders

Creatures Moving
Edited by Geoffrey Summerfield

Stage Two
Danger!
Edited by Norman Beer (spring 1977)

Good Time
Edited by Margaret Hewitt

Openings
Edited by Alex McLeod

The Receiving End
Edited by Peter Medway

That Once was Me
Edited by Dennis Pepper

Alone
Edited by George Robertson

Stage Three
Identity
Edited by Myra Barrs

Making Contact . . . and Breaking It
Edited by Pat D'Arcy (spring 1977)

The English Projec

Taki
being taken
BEING THE
LAID INTO WRONG END OF
Taking HAVIN
Getting what was you a Hammering
coming to
BEING DESSEM ABOUT gettin
getting being seen coming
a Larruping Taking
making your bed and having to lie on it be
getting taken down a peg gettir
being shown the door
getting conned GETTIN

Edited by Peter Medway

Stage Two **The Receiving End**

getting taken for a ride

come

HOCKEY

coming well unstuck

k S.

ROUGH PASSAGE

having the piss took

S. getting well

slaughtered

d up the

ARDEN path taking copping it

asting aknock

BEING HAD

being made to look a right charlie

de a monkey

GETTING CUT

one DOWN TO SIZE

ng shown where to get off getting sorted

GOOD HIDING out

Ward Lock Educational

First published as the Penguin English Project
by Penguin Books 1973
This edition published by Ward Lock Educational 1976
This selection copyright © Peter Medway 1976

ISBN 0 7062 3533 9

Designed by Ivan Atanasoff
Set in Monophoto Apollo
by Oliver Burridge Filmsetting Ltd, Crawley
and printed by Ebenezer Baylis and Son, Worcester
for Ward Lock Educational
116 Baker Street, London W1M 2BB
Made in Great Britain

Contents

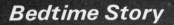

Bedtime Story

Nighttime. The faithful prison guard,
Poverty, locks the Negroes in their neighbourhoods.
And many white men seal themselves
in the condemned buildings of the soul.

America sleeps, the raw wounds still open.
Mississippi sheriffs enter and stalk
in the forests of dreams; Southern judges,
pounding their gavels, crush small eyes in the brain.

On a highway, a good man is overtaken
by a carload of hoodlums.
Turn away quick!
or you'll see him get it.

Goodnight.

Lou Lipsitz

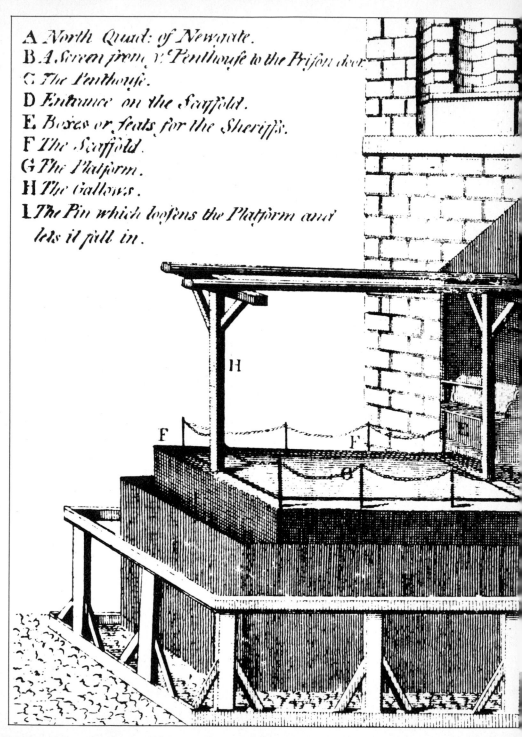

A *North Quad: of Newgate.*

B. *A Screen from y.ᵉ Penthouse to the Prison door.*

C *The Penthouse.*

D *Entrance on the Scaffold.*

E *Boxes or seats for the Sheriffs.*

F *The Scaffold.*

G *The Platform.*

H *The Gallows.*

I *The Pin which loosens the Platform and lets it fall in.*

The Hangman

Into our town the hangman came,
Smelling of gold and blood and flame –
And he paced our bricks with a diffident air
And built his frame on the courthouse square.

The scaffold stood by the courthouse side,
Only as wide as the door was wide;
A frame as tall, or little more,
Than the capping sill of the courthouse door.

And we wondered, whenever we had the time,
Who the criminal, what the crime.
The Hangman judged with the yellow twist
Of knotted hemp in his busy fist.

And innocent though we were, with dread
We passed those eyes of buckshot lead;
Till one cried, 'Hangman! Who is he
For whom you raise the gallows-tree?'

Then a twinkle grew in the buckshot eye
And he gave us a riddle instead of reply:
'He who serves me best,' said he,
'Shall earn the rope on the gallows-tree.'

And he stepped down, and laid his hand
On a man who came from another land –
And we breathed again, for another's grief
At the Hangman's hand was our relief.

And the gallows-frame on the courthouse lawn
By tomorrow's sun would be struck and gone.
So we gave him way, and no one spoke
Out of respect for his hangman's cloak.

The next day's sun looked mildly down
On roof and street in our quiet town
And, stark and black in the morning air
The gallows-tree on the courthouse square.

And the Hangman stood at his usual stand
With the yellow hemp in his busy hand;
With his buckshot eye and his jaw like a pike
And his air so knowing and businesslike.

11

And we cried, 'Hangman, have you not done'
Yesterday, with the alien one?'
Then he fell silent, and stood amazed:
Oh, not for him was the gallows raised. . . .'

He laughed a laugh as he looked at us:
. . . Did you think I'd gone to all this fuss
To hang one man? That's a thing I do
To stretch the rope when the rope is new.'

Then one cried 'Murderer!' One cried 'Shame!'
And into our midst the Hangman came
To that man's place. 'Do you hold,' said he,
With him that was meat for the gallows-tree?'

And he laid his hand on that one's arm,
And we shrank back in quick alarm,
And we gave him way, and no one spoke
Out of the fear for his hangman's cloak.

That night we saw with dread surprise
The Hangman's scaffold had grown in size.
Fed by the blood beneath the chute
The gallows-tree had taken root;

Now it was wide, and a little more,
Than the steps which led to the courthouse door,
And tall as the writing, or nearly as tall,
Halfway up on the courthouse wall.

The third he took – we had all heard tell –
A usurer and an infidel,
And: 'What,' said the Hangman, 'have you to do
With the gallows-bound, and he a Jew?'

And we cried out, 'Is this one he
Who has served you well and faithfully?'
The Hangman smiled, 'It's a clever scheme
To try the strength of the gallows-beam.'

The fourth man's dark accusing song
Had scratched our comfort hard and long;
And: 'What concern,' he gave us back,
Have you for the doomed – the doomed and black?'

The fifth. The sixth. And we cried again:
Hangman! Hangman, is this the man?'
It's a trick,' he said, 'that we hangmen know
For easing the trap when the trap springs slow.'

And so we ceased, and asked no more,
As the Hangman tallied his bloody score;
And sun by sun, and night by night,
The gallows grew to monstrous height.

The wings of the scaffold opened wide
Till they covered the square from side to side;
And the monster cross-beam, looking down,
Cast its shadow across the town.

Then through the town the Hangman came
And called in the empty streets my name –
And I looked at the gallows soaring tall
And thought, 'There's no one left at all

For hanging, and so he calls to me
To help pull down the gallows-tree.'
And I went out with right good hope
To the Hangman's tree and the Hangman's rope.

He smiled at me as I came down
To the courthouse square through the silent town,
And supple and stretched in his busy hand
Was the yellow twist of the hempen strand

And he whistled his tune as he tried the trap
And it sprang down with a ready snap –
And then with a smile of awful command,
He laid his hand upon my hand.

'You tricked me, Hangman!' I shouted then,
'That your scaffold was built for other men. . .
And I no henchman of yours,' I cried,
'You lied to me, Hangman, foully lied!'

Then a twinkle grew in the buckshot eye:
'Lied to you? Tricked you?' he said, 'Not I.
For I answered straight and I told you true:
The scaffold was raised for none but you.

'For who has served more faithfully
Than you with your coward's hope?' said he,
'And where are the others who might have stood
Side by your side in the common good?'

'Dead,' I whispered; and amiably
'Murdered,' the Hangman corrected me:
'First the alien, then the Jew. . . .
I did no more than you let me do.'

Beneath the beam that blocked the sky,
None had stood so alone as I –
And the Hangman strapped me, and no voice there
Cried, 'Stay!' for me in the empty square.

Maurice Ogden

A Protestant Minister Speaks at his Trial in Nazi Germany

First they came to fetch the Communists; I did not speak because I was not a Communist. Then they came to fetch the workers, members of trade unions; I did not speak because I was not a working member of a trade union. Afterwards, they came to fetch the Catholics and the Jews; I did not say anything because I was a Protestant. Eventually they came to fetch me, and nobody was left to speak.

Anonymous

This String Business

The conductor kept knocking at his driver's window and dangling a piece of string. After he'd done it several times, a passenger said, 'What's the string business?'

He said, 'Oh just a little joke, Guv.'

The passenger said, 'Your driver doesn't seem to think so, he's looking daggers at you.'

The conductor said, 'E ain't got much sense of humour.'

The passenger said, 'Well . . . what's it all about?'

The conductor said, 'I's old man was 'UNG this morning.'

Anonymous

The Arrest

Someone must have been telling lies about Joseph K., for without having done anything wrong he was arrested one fine morning. His landlady's cook, who always brought him his breakfast at eight o'clock, failed to appear on this occasion. That had never happened before. K. waited for a little longer, watching from his pillow the old lady opposite, who seemed to be peering at him with a curiosity unusual even for her, but then, feeling both put out and hungry, he rang the bell. At once there was a knock at the door and a man entered whom he had never seen before in the house. He was slim and yet well knit, he wore a closely fitting black suit, which was furnished with all sorts of pleats, pockets, buckles and buttons, as well as a belt, like a tourist's outfit, and in consequence looked eminently practical, though one could not quite tell what actual purpose it served. 'Who are you?' asked K., half raising himself in bed. But the man ignored the question, as though his appearance needed no explanation, and merely said: 'Did you ring?' 'Anna is to bring me my breakfast,' said K., and then with silent intensity studied the fellow, trying to make out who he could be. The man did not submit to this scrutiny for very long, but turned to the door and opened it slightly so as to report to someone who was evidently standing just behind it: 'He says Anna is to bring him his breakfast.' A short guffaw from the next room came in answer; one could not tell from the sound whether it was produced by several individuals or merely by one. Although the strange man could not have learned anything from it that he did not know already, he now said to K., as if passing on a statement: 'It can't be done.' 'This is news indeed,' cried K., springing out of bed and quickly pulling on his trousers. 'I must see what people these are next door, and how Frau Grubach can account to me for such behaviour.' Yet it occurred to him at once that he should not have said this aloud and that by doing so he had in a way admitted the stranger's right to an interest in his actions; still, that did not seem important to him at the moment. The stranger, however, took his words in some such sense, for he asked: 'Hadn't you better stay here?' 'I shall neither stay here nor let you address me until you have introduced yourself.' 'I meant well enough,' said the stranger, and then of his own accord threw the door open. In the next room, which K. entered more slowly than he had intended, everything looked at first glance almost as it had done the evening before. It was Frau Grubach's living-room; perhaps among all the furniture, rugs, china and photographs with which it was crammed there was a little more free space than usual, yet one did not perceive that at first, especially as the main change consisted in the presence of a man who was sitting at the open window reading a book, from which he now glanced up. 'You should have stayed in your room! Didn't Franz tell you that?' 'Yes, yes, but what are you doing here?' asked K., looking from his new acquaintance to the man called Franz, who was still standing by the door, and then back again. Through the open window he had another glimpse of the old woman, who with truly senile inquisitiveness had moved along to the window exactly opposite, in order to see all that could be seen. 'I'd better get Frau Grubach . . .' said K., as if wrenching himself away from the two men (though they were standing at quite a distance from him) and making as if to go out. 'No,' said the man at the window, flinging the book down on the table and getting up. 'You can't go out, you are arrested.' 'So it seems,' said K. 'But what for?' he added. 'We are not authorized to tell you that. Go to your room and wait there. Proceedings have been instituted against you, and you will be informed of everything in due course. I am exceeding my instructions in speaking freely to you like this. But I hope nobody hears me except Franz, and he himself has been too free with you, against his express instructions. If you continue to have as good luck as you have had in the choice of your warders, then you can be confident of the final result.' K. felt he must sit down, but now he saw that there was no seat in the whole room except the chair beside the window. 'You'll soon discover that we're telling you the truth,' said Franz, advancing towards him simultaneously with the other man. The latter overtopped K. enormously and kept clapping him on the shoulder. They both examined his nightshirt and said that he would have to wear a less fancy shirt now, but that they would take charge of this one and the rest of his underwear and, if his case turned out well, restore them to him later. 'Much better give these things to us than hand them over to the depot,' they said, 'for in the depot there's lots of thieving, and besides they sell everything there after a certain length of time, no matter whether your case is settled or not. And you never know how long these cases will last, especially these days. Of course you would get the money out of the depot in the long run, but in the first place the prices they pay you are always wretched, for they sell your things to the best briber, not the best bidder, and anyhow it's well known that money dwindles a lot if it passes from hand to hand from one year to another.' K. paid hardly any attention to this advice, any right to dispose of his own things which he might possess he did not prize very highly; far more important to him was the necessity to understand his situation clearly; but with these people beside him he could not even think, the belly of the second warder – for they could only be warders – kept butting against him in an almost friendly way, yet if he looked up he caught sight of a face which did not in the least suit that fat body, a dry, bony face with a great nose, twisted to one side, which seemed to be consulting over his head with the other warder. Who could these men be? What were they talking about? What authority could they represent? K. lived in a country with a legal constitution, there was universal peace, all the laws were in force; who dared seize him in his own dwelling? . . .

But he was still free. 'Allow me,' he said, passing quickly between the warders to his room. 'He seems to have some sense,' he heard one of them saying behind him. When he reached his room he at once pulled out the drawer of his desk, everything lay there in perfect order, but in his agitation he could not find at first the identification papers for which he was looking. At last he found his bicycle licence and was about to start off with it to the warders, but then it seemed too trivial a thing, and he searched again until he found his birth certificate. As he was re-entering the next room the opposite door opened and Frau Grubach showed herself. He saw her only for an instant, for no sooner did she recognize him than she was obviously overcome by embarrassment, apologized for intruding, vanished, and shut the door again with the utmost care. 'Come in, do,' he would just have had time to say. But he merely stood holding his papers in the middle of the room, looking at the door, which did not open again, and was only recalled to attention by a shout from the warders, who were sitting at a table by the open window and, as he now saw, devouring his breakfast. 'Why didn't she come in?' he asked. 'She isn't allowed to,' said the tall warder, 'since you're under arrest.' 'But how can I be under arrest? And particularly in such a ridiculous fashion?' 'So now you're beginning it all over again?' said the warder, dipping a slice of bread and butter into the honey-pot. 'We don't answer such questions.' 'You'll have to answer them,' said K. 'Here are my papers, now show me yours, and first of all your warrant for arresting me.' 'Oh, good Lord,' said the warder. 'If you would only realize your position, and if you wouldn't insist on uselessly annoying us two, who probably mean better by you and stand closer to you than any other people in the world.' 'That's so, you can believe that,' said Franz, not raising to his lips the coffee-cup he held in his hand, but instead giving K. a long, apparently significant, yet incomprehensible look. Without wishing it K. found himself decoyed into an exchange of speaking looks with Franz, none the less he tapped his papers and repeated: 'Here are my identification papers.' 'What are your papers to us?' cried the tall warder. 'You're behaving worse than a child. What are you after? Do you think you'll bring this fine case of yours to a speedier end by wrangling with us, your warders, over papers and warrants? We are humble subordinates who can scarcely find our way through a legal document and have nothing to do with your case except to stand guard over you for ten hours a day and draw our pay for it. That's all we are, but we're quite capable of grasping the fact that the high authorities we serve, before they would order such an arrest as this must be quite well informed about the reasons for the arrest and the person of the prisoner. There can be no mistake about that. Our officials, so far as I know them, and I know only the lowest grades among them, never go hunting for crime in the populace, but, as the Law decrees, are drawn towards the guilty and must then send out us warders. That is the Law. How could there be a mistake in that?'

'I don't know this Law,' said K. 'All the worse for you,' replied the warder.

Franz Kafka The Trial. *Translated from the German by Willa and Edwin Muir*

Sentence

'... anything to say before sentence is passed on you?'...

'No, my Lord. I wish to add nothing to what I have already said.'...
The judge has started to speak, and I look back at him. I am glad he
is looking at me. I do not know it, but in the years to come I am to
appear before men who will be adjudicating some trivial breach of
prison rules. There will not be sufficient evidence before them to
convict a dog, but they will convict just the same, and when they
convict they will gabble their verdict and their sentence of so many
days' bread and water, so many days' loss of pay and privileges.
And while they gabble out the routine words of punishment, they
will look anywhere but into the eyes of the man they are trying.
They will not all be like that. I shall meet at least one who will
punish with insufficient evidence, because he has to, because the
system would fall down if he did not. But he will look squarely at
the man in front of him when he does it, and his blue eyes will be sad.

'... alternative to sentence you to life imprisonment.'

I do not know what I am still waiting for. Perhaps it is that, knowing
the climax in advance, I wait for something else, something more
stupendous and mind-shattering than those few words, quietly
spoken, 'life imprisonment'.

I glance quickly round the court again. Everyone has become
suddenly very busy. With heads down, counsel, solicitors and
clerks shuffle and sort papers, whispering to each other in asides,
glancing about them – anywhere but at me. It seems they are ashamed
of the part they have played in theoretically disposing of a man's
body for the rest of his life. I am to be told later that when a man has
been sentenced to death the court's embarrassment becomes so
infectious that even police and prison officers avoid each other's
eyes for some minutes, until they summon up a piece of bluff
repartee which rings so patently insincere that the embarrassment
is only increased.

I feel a tug at my sleeve and I look at the officer on my left. He mouths
two words at me.

'Right. Down.'

Zeno *A Life*

Taken to a Cell

Then I was taken to a cell.

For the first time I heard the sound of a cell door being slammed from the outside.

It is a unique sound. A cell door has no handle, either outside or inside; it cannot be shut except by being slammed to. It is made of massive steel and concrete, about four inches thick, and every time it falls to there is a resounding crash just as though a shot has been fired. But this report dies away without an echo. Prison sounds are echo-less and bleak.

When the door has been slammed behind him for the first time, the prisoner stands in the middle of the cell and looks round. I fancy that everyone must behave in more or less the same way.

First of all he gives a fleeting look round the walls and takes a mental inventory of all the objects in what is now to be his domain:

the iron bedstead,
the wash-basin,
the W.C.,
the barred window.

His next action is invariably to try to pull himself up by the iron bars of the window and look out. He fails, and his suit is covered with white from the plaster on the wall against which he has pressed himself.

He desists, but decides to practise and master the art of pulling himself up by his hands. Indeed, he makes all sorts of laudable resolutions; he will do exercises every morning and learn a foreign language, and he simply won't let his spirit be broken. He dusts his suit and continues his voyage of exploration round his puny realm – five paces long by four paces broad. He tries the iron bedstead. The springs are broken, the wire mattress sags and cuts into the flesh; it's like lying in a hammock made of steel wire. He pulls a face, being determined to prove that he is full of courage and confidence. Then his gaze rests on the cell door, and he sees that an eye is glued to the spy-hole and is watching him.

The eye goggles at him glassily, its pupil unbelievably big; it is an eye without a man attached to it, and for a few moments the prisoner's heart stops beating.

The eye disappears and the prisoner takes a deep breath and presses his hand against the left side of his chest.

'Now, then,' he says to himself encouragingly, 'how silly to go and get so frightened. You must get used to that; after all, the official's only doing his duty by peeping in; that's part of being in prison. But they won't get me down; I'll stuff paper in the spy-hole at night. . . .'

As a matter of fact there's no reason why he shouldn't do so straight away. The idea fills him with genuine enthusiasm. For the first time he experiences that almost maniac desire for activity that from now on will alternate continually – up and down in a never-ending zig-zag – with melancholia and depression.

Then he realizes that he has no paper on him, and his next impulse is – according to his social status – either to ring or to run over to the stationer's at the corner. This impulse lasts only the fraction of a second; the next moment he becomes conscious for the first time of the true significance of his situation. For the first time he grasps the full reality of being behind a door which is locked from outside, grasps it in all its searing, devastating poignancy.

This, too, lasts only a few seconds. The next moment the anaesthetizing mechanism gets going again, and brings about that merciful state of semi-narcosis induced by pacing up and down, forging plans, weaving illusions.

'Let's see,' says the novice, 'where were we? Ah, yes, that business of stuffing paper in the spy-hole. It *must* be possible to get hold of paper somehow or other.' He leaves the 'how' in this 'somehow' suspended in mid-air. This is a mode of thought that he will soon master – or, rather it will master him. 'When I get out,' he will say for example, 'I shall never worry about money again. I shall run along somehow or other.' Or: 'When I get out, I shall never quarrel with the wife again. We'll manage to get along somehow.'

Indeed, 'somehow or other' everything will be all right once he's free.

The fact that the prisoner follows this stereotyped line of thought, which, as I say, is going, after a few days, to master him, means that the outside world increasingly loses its reality for him; it becomes a dream world in which everything is somehow or other possible.

'Where were we?... Oh, yes, that business of stuffing paper in the spy-hole. Of course, somehow or other one can get hold of some paper. But is it allowed? No, it's certain not to be allowed. So why bother?...

'Let's take a more thorough inventory of the objects in the room. Why, look, there's an iron table with a chair which we haven't observed or fully appreciated yet. Of course the chair can't be moved from the table; it's welded to it. A pity, otherwise one might use it as a bed table and put one's things on it when getting undressed – pocket-book, handkerchief, cigarettes, matches and so on ....'

Then it occurs to him that he has neither pocket-book nor handkerchief, cigarettes nor matches in his pocket.

The barometer of his mood falls a second time.

It rises again the moment he has tried the tap over the wash-basin. Look, there's running water in prison – it isn't half as bad as one imagined from outside. After all, there is a bed (and it's much healthier to sleep on a hard bed), a wash-basin, a table, a chair – what more does a man need? One must learn to live simply and unassumingly: a few exercises, reading, writing, learning a foreign language. . . .'

The next voyage of discovery is in the direction of the water closet. 'Why, there's even one of these – it's really not half so bad.' He pulls the plug. The chain refuses to function. And the barometer falls afresh.

It rises again once the subtle plan has been conceived of filling the bucket with water from the tap and of flushing the lavatory pan in this way. It falls again when it transpires that the tap has also ceased to function. It rises again when he reflects that there must be certain times of the day when the water runs. It falls – it rises – it falls – it rises. And this is how things are to go on – in the coming minutes, hours, days, weeks, years.

How long has he already been in the cell?

He looks at his watch: exactly three minutes.

Arthur Koestler *Dialogue With Death*

Prison Comforts

Warder Regan comes on with a bottle marked 'methylated spirit'.

WARDER REGAN You're the two for rubs, for your rheumatism.

DUNLAVIN That's right, Mr Regan sir, old and bet, sir, that's us.
And the old pains is very bad with us these times, sir.

WARDER REGAN Not so much lip, and sit down whoever is first for
treatment.

DUNLAVIN That's me, sir. Age before ignorance, as the man said.
[Sits in the chair]

WARDER REGAN Rise the leg of your trousers. Which leg is it?

DUNLAVIN The left, sir.

WARDER REGAN That's the right leg you're showing me.

DUNLAVIN That's what I was saying, sir. The left is worst one day
and the right is bad the next. To be on the safe side, you'd have
to do two of them. It's only the mercy of God I'm not a centipede,
sir, with the weather that's in it.

WARDER REGAN Is that where the pain is?

DUNLAVIN *[bending down slowly towards the bottle]* A little lower
down, sir, if you please. *[Grabs the bottle and raises it to his
mouth]* Just a little lower down, sir, if it's all equal to you.
*[Regan rubs, head well bent, and Dunlavin drinks long and deeply and
as quickly lowers the bottle on to the floor again, wiping his mouth
and making the most frightful grimaces, for the stuff doesn't go
down easy at first. He goes through the pantomime of being burnt
inside for Neighbour's benefit and rubs his mouth with the back of
his hand]*

DUNLAVIN Ah, that's massive, sir. 'Tis you that has the healing
hand. You must have desperate luck at the horses; I'd only love
to be with you copying your dockets. *[Regan turns and pours more
spirit on his hands]* Ah, that's it, sir, well into me I can feel it
going. *[Reaches forward towards the bottle again, drinks]* Ah,
that's it, I can feel it going right into me. And doing me all the
good in the world. *[Regan reaches and puts more spirit on his hand
and sets to rubbing again]* That's it, sir, thorough does it; if you're
going to do a thing at all you might as well do it well. *[Reaches
forward for the bottle again and raises it. Neighbour looks across in
piteous appeal to him not to drink so much, but he merely waves the
bottle in elegant salute, as if to wish him good health, and takes
another drink]* May God reward you, sir, you must be the seventh
son of the seventh son of one of the Lees from Limerick on your
mother's side maybe. *[Drinks again]* Ah, that's the cure for the
cold of the wind and the world's neglectment.

WARDER REGAN Right, now you.

Brendan Behan *The Quare Fellow*

26

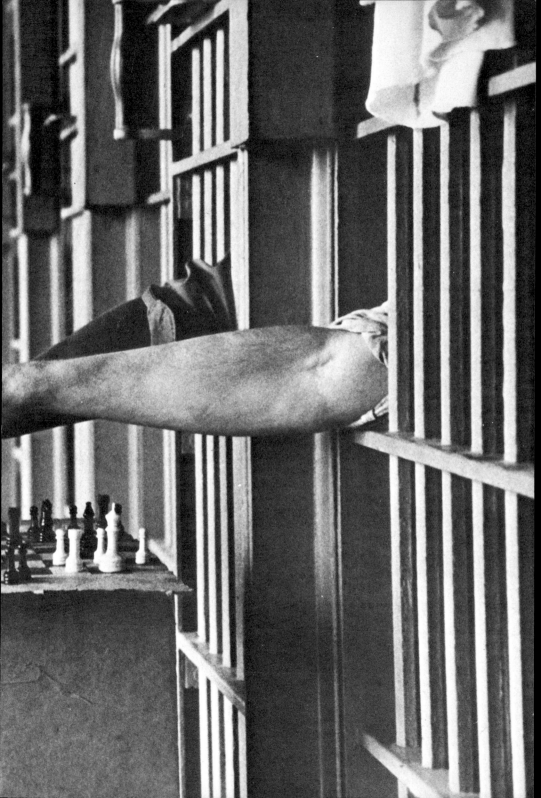

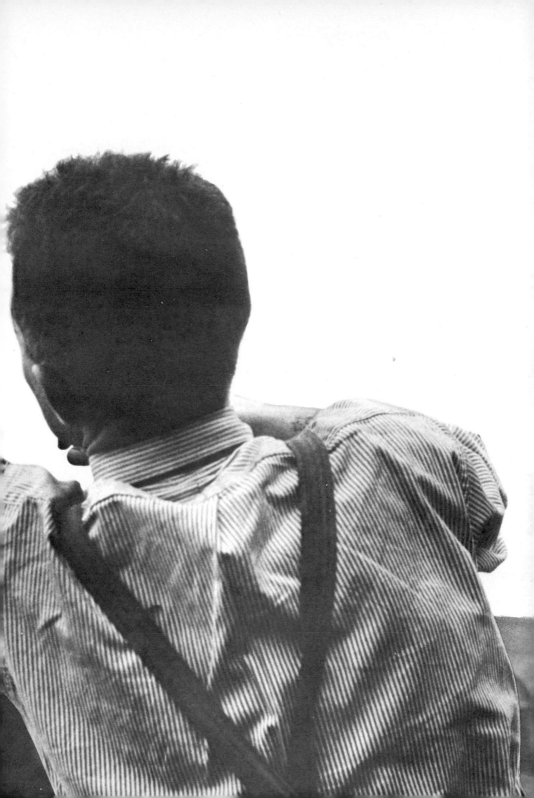

P.O.W.

(It is nearly the end of the Second World War in Europe. A group of American prisoners arrive at a German prison camp after a long train journey during which they have been brutally treated and some have died. They are all ordinary GIs, not officers. One of them is Billy Pilgrim.)

Properly enrolled and tagged, the Americans were led through gate after gate again. In two days' time now their families would learn from the International Red Cross that they were alive. . . .

'Halt,' said a guard.

The Americans halted. They stood there quietly in the cold.

The sheds they were among were outwardly like thousands of other sheds they had passed. There was this difference, though: the sheds had tin chimneys, and out of the chimneys whirled constellations of sparks.

A guard knocked on a door.

The door was flung open from inside. Light leaped out through the door, escaped from prison at 186,000 miles per second. Out marched fifty middle-aged Englishmen. They were singing 'Hail, Hail, the Gang's All Here' from *The Pirates of Penzance*.

These lusty, ruddy vocalists were among the first English-speaking prisoners to be taken in the Second World War. Now they were singing to nearly the last. They had not seen a woman or a child for four years or more. They hadn't seen any birds, either. Not even sparrows would come into the camp.

The Englishmen were officers. Each of them had attempted to escape from another prison at least once. Now they were here, dead-centre in a sea of dying Russians.

They could tunnel all they pleased. They would inevitably surface within a rectangle of barbed wire, would find themselves greeted listlessly by dying Russians who spoke no English, who had no food or useful information or escape plans of their own. They could scheme all they pleased to hide aboard a vehicle or steal one, but no vehicle ever came into their compound. They could feign illness if they liked, but that wouldn't earn them a trip anywhere, either. The only hospital in the camp was a six-bed affair in the British compound itself.

The Englishmen were clean and enthusiastic and decent and strong. They sang boomingly well. They had been singing together every night for years.

The Englishmen had also been lifting weights and chinning themselves for years. Their bellies were like washboards. The muscles of their calves and upper arms were like cannonballs. They were all masters of checkers and chess and cribbage and dominoes and anagrams and charades and ping-pong and billiards, as well.

They were among the wealthiest people in Europe, in terms of food. A clerical error early in the war, when food was still getting through to prisoners, had caused the Red Cross to ship them five hundred parcels every month instead of fifty. The Englishmen had hoarded these so cunningly that now, as the war was ending, they had three tons of sugar, one ton of coffee, eleven hundred pounds of chocolate, seven hundred pounds of tobacco, seventeen hundred pounds of tea, two tons of flour, one ton of canned beef, twelve hundred pounds of canned butter, sixteen hundred pounds of canned cheese, eight hundred pounds of powdered milk, and two tons of orange marmalade.

They kept all this in a room without windows. They had ratproofed it by lining it with flattened tin cans.

They were adored by the Germans, who thought they were exactly what Englishmen ought to be. They made war look stylish and reasonable, and fun. So the Germans let them have four sheds, though one shed would have held them all. And, in exchange for coffee or chocolate or tobacco, the Germans gave them paint and lumber and nails and cloth for fixing things up.

The Englishmen had known for twelve hours that American guests were on their way. They had never had guests before, and they went to work like darling elves, sweeping, mopping, cooking, baking – making mattresses of straw and burlap bags, setting tables, putting party favours at each place.

Now they were singing their welcome to their guests in the winter night. Their clothes were aromatic with the feast they had been preparing. They were dressed half for battle, half for tennis or croquet. They were so elated by their own hospitality, and by all the goodies waiting inside, that they did not take a good look at their guests while they sang. And they imagined they were singing to fellow officers fresh from the fray.

They wrestled the Americans toward the shed door affectionately, boasting filling the night with manly blather and brotherly rodomontades. They called them "Yank," told them "Good show," promised them that "Jerry was on the run," and so on.

Billy Pilgrim wondered dimly who Jerry was.

Now he was inside, next to an iron cookstove that was glowing cherry red. Dozens of teapots were boiling there. Some of them had whistles. And there was a witches' cauldron full of golden soup. The soup was thick. Primeval bubbles surfaced it with lethargical majesty as Billy Pilgrim stared.

There were long tables set for a banquet. At each place was a bowl made from a can that had once contained powdered milk. A smaller can was a cup. A taller, more slender can, was a tumbler. Each tumbler was filled with warm milk.

At each place was a safety razor, a washcloth, a package of razor blades, a chocolate bar, two cigars, a bar of soap, ten cigarettes, a book of matches, a pencil and a candle.

Only the candles and the soap were of German origin. They had a ghostly, opalescent similarity. The British had no way of knowing it, but the candles and the soap were made from the fat of rendered Jews and gypsies and fairies and communists, and other enemies of the state.

So it goes.

The banquet hall was illuminated by candlelight. There were heaps of fresh-baked white bread on the tables, gobs of butter, pots of marmalade. There were platters of sliced beef from cans. Soup and scrambled eggs and hot marmalade pie were yet to come.

And, at the far end of the shed, Billy saw pink arches with azure draperies hanging between them, and an enormous clock, and two golden thrones, and a bucket and a mop. It was in this setting that the evening's entertainment would take place, a musical version of *Cinderella*, the most popular story ever told.

dry wood Billy Pilgrim was on fire, having stood too close to the glowing stove. The hem of his little coat was burning. It was a quiet, patient sort of fire – like the burning of punk.

Billy wondered if there was a telephone somewhere. He wanted to call his mother, to tell her he was alive and well.

There was silence now, as the Englishmen looked in astonishment at the frowsy creatures they had so lustily waltzed inside. One of the Englishmen saw that Billy was on fire. 'You're on fire, lad!' he said, and got Billy away from the stove and beat out the sparks with his hands.

When Billy made no comment on this, the Englishman asked him, 'Can you talk? Can you hear?'

Billy nodded.

The Englishman touched him exploratorily here and there, filled with pity. 'My God – what have they done to you, lad? This isn't a man. It's a broken kite.'

'Are you really an American?' said the Englishman.

'Yes,' said Billy.

'And your rank?'

'Private.'

'What became of your boots, lad?'

'I don't remember.'

'Is that coat a *joke*?'

'Sir?'

'Where did you get such a thing?'

Billy had to think hard about that. 'They gave it to me,' he said at last.

'Jerry gave it to you?'

'Who?'

'The Germans gave it to you?'

'Yes.'

Billy didn't like the questions. They were fatiguing.

'Ohhhh – Yank, Yank, Yank –' said the Englishman, 'that coat was an *insult*.'

'Sir?'

'It was a deliberate attempt to humiliate you. You mustn't let Jerry do things like that.'

Billy Pilgrim swooned.

Billy came to on a chair facing the stage. He had somehow eaten, and now he was watching *Cinderella*. Some part of him had evidently been enjoying the performance for quite a while. Billy was laughing loud.

The women in the play were really men, of course. The clock had just struck midnight, and Cinderella was lamenting:

'Goodness me, the clock has struck –
Alackaday, and fuck my luck.'

Billy found the couplet so comical that he not only laughed – he shrieked. He went on shrieking until he was carried out of the shed and into another, where the hospital was. It was a six-bed hospital. There weren't any other patients in there.

Kurt Vonnegut *Slaughterhouse Five*

The Deepest Pain

The deepest pain of a prisoner's life is a constant, faint trickling sound at the back of his mind of the sands of his life running out. Sometimes it becomes a roar like an avalanche. I heard this avalanche for a minute or two in Benghazi when five of my teeth came out one morning.

René Cutforth *Order to View*

General, That Tank

General, that tank of yours is some car.
It can wreck a forest, crush a hundred men.
But it has one failing:
It needs a driver.

General, you've got a good bomber there.
It can fly faster than the wind, carry more
    than an elephant can.
But it has one failing:
It needs a mechanic.

General, a man is a useful creature.
He can fly, and he can kill.
But he has one failing:
He can think.

Bertolt Brecht *Translated from the German
by Christopher Middleton*

Army Medicine – First World War, Austrian Empire Style

At this momentous epoch the great concern of the military doctors was to drive the devil of sabotage out of the malingerers and persons suspected of being malingerers, such as consumptives, sufferers from rheumatism, rupture, kidney disease, diabetes, inflammation of the lungs, and other disorders.

The torments to which malingerers were subjected had been reduced to a system, and the degrees of torment were as follows:

1. Absolute diet – a cup of tea morning and evening for three days, accompanied by doses of aspirin to produce sweating, irrespective of what the patient complained of.

2. To prevent them from supposing that the army was all beer and skittles, they were given ample doses of quinine in powder.

3. Rinsing of the stomach twice daily with a litre of warm water.

syringe inserted in the rectum 4. The use of the clyster with soapy water and glycerine.

5. Swathing in sheets soaked with cold water.

There were dauntless persons who went through all five degrees of torment and had themselves removed in a simple coffin to the military cemetery. There were, however, others who were faint-hearted and who, when they reached the clyster stage, announced that they were quite well and that their only desire was to proceed to the trenches with the next draft.

On reaching the military prison, Schweik was placed in the hut used as an infirmary which contained several of these faint-hearted malingerers.

'I can't stand it any longer,' said his bed-neighbour, who had been brought in from the surgery where his stomach had been rinsed for the second time.

This man was pretending to be shortsighted.

'I'm going to join my regiment,' decided the other malingerer on Schweik's left, who had just had a taste of the clyster, after pretending to be as deaf as a post.

On the bed by the door a consumptive was dying, wrapped up in a sheet soaked in cold water.

'That's the third this week,' remarked Schweik's right-hand neighbour. 'And what's wrong with you?'

'I've got rheumatism,' replied Schweik, whereupon there was hearty laughter from all those round about him. Even the dying consumptive, who was pretending to have tuberculosis, laughed.

'It's no good coming here with rheumatism,' said a stout man to Schweik in solemn tones, 'rheumatism here stands about as much chance as corns. I'm anaemic, half my stomach's missing and I've lost five ribs, but nobody believes me. Why, we actually had a deaf and dumb man here, and every half hour they wrapped him up in sheets soaked in cold water, and every day they gave him a taste of the clyster and pumped his stomach out. Just when all the ambulance men thought he'd done the trick and would get away with it, the doctor prescribed some medicine for him. That fairly doubled him up, and then he gave in. "No," he says, "I can't go on with this deaf and dumb business, my speech and hearing have been restored to me." The sick chaps all told him not to do for himself like that, but he said no, he could hear and talk just like the others. And when the doctor came in the morning, he reported himself accordingly.'

Jaroslav Hašek *The Good Soldier Schweik. Translated from the Czech by Paul Selver*

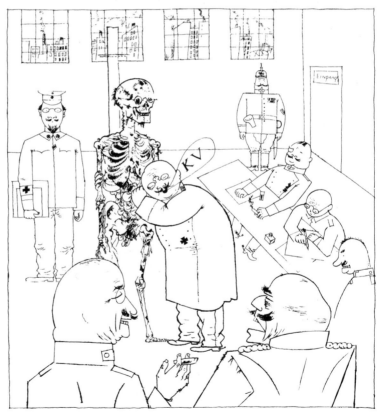

KV = *kriegsverwendungsfähig* – fit for active duty

Hamp is Questioned about Desertion by his Defending Officer, Desertion Carrying the Death Penalty

CORPORAL Prisoner! Halt!

HARGREAVES All right. Stand easy. Stand by again in the Guard Room, Corporal.

CORPORAL [*Saluting*] Sir. [*He and Guard go out*]

HARGREAVES Now, Hamp, sit down. To get back to the point. I asked you – did you not *expect* to be arrested?

HAMP It's same as I never thought about it, sir, one way or t'other.

HARGREAVES Yes, all right. Leave that for the moment. But can you tell my *why* you desert – why you went absent?

HAMP I couldn't stand it no more, sir.

HARGREAVES But surely, man! I mean, why this time? After all you've been through –

HAMP It weren't the first time I thought about doing it, sir.

HARGREAVES What?

HAMP I nearly did it once afore, sir. I thought about it. It were time of Arras. I were sent back one time there on a water party. I were thinking about running away, but a Redcap got 'is eye on me, so I didn't.

HARGREAVES And that was all?

HAMP Yes, sir.

HARGREAVES Forget about that too. Put it out of your mind.

HAMP Yes, sir.

HARGREAVES But I want to know more about this time. Much more. I have to know. About how it happened and about the reasons and thoughts and motives that were in your mind.

HAMP Same as I said, sir, I don't know no more to tell you. I couldn't stand it no more.

HARGREAVES But you're a soldier, man. You've got to stand it. You stood it all the other times.

HAMP I'm not saying there were sense in it, sir, but –

HARGREAVES Suppose your comrades had ever run away and left *you* to it – say, at Loos, or Trones Wood – you'd have been in a fine mess, wouldn't you?

HAMP [*After thinking about this*] I don't think it could've been much worse nor it were, sir – and that's the God's truth.
[*Hargreaves is momentarily silenced by this*]

HARGREAVES All right. Now, from the beginning, tell me what happened.

HAMP Well, I were in that attack, sir. It were very bad.

HARGREAVES Yes, I know.

HAMP Didn't get wounded – but the time when this came into my head were – I got blown into a shell-hole. It were a deep one, deepest muck ever I saw. I thought I were done for, sure – getting sucked down into t'muck. Only just when I were going right under two of the lads saw it. They gave me butt-end of a rifle and they pulled me out. It's not sense, sir, but that were worse nor anything else that ever came on me afore. It were same as I couldn't get over it, like. I couldn't stand it no more – after.

HARGREAVES But you got out of it all right. And surely it was some time after that attack when you – I mean, it wasn't a case of running away in panic from the front line. After that attack, as I understand it, your battalion was relieved. You were sent back for a rest.

HAMP Yes, sir. A bit back.

HARGREAVES And it was from there, about ten days after the attack, that you deserted.

HAMP Yes, sir.

HARGREAVES Why? Why then?

HAMP Same as I said, sir. I couldn't stand no more.

HARGREAVES You mean that from the time of the attack, and your – from the time when you had that bad shock in the shell-hole, you were in a continual state of fear. Is that what you mean?

HAMP I think that's right, sir.

HARGREAVES *Is* that what you mean? Thinking is not good enough. I've got to know. Was this something worse than the normal feeling of fear before you went into action?

HAMP Honest, sir – it were worse, worse nor anything.

HARGREAVES [*After waiting for him to say more*] Yes? Please try to tell me. This is what I want to know, in your own words.

HAMP It were same as I – after the attack – after I got out o' that shell-'ole – I were different, sir. Like – different in myself.

HARGREAVES Yes? Tell me. In what way? This is important to you, I promise you. In what way different?
[*There is a long, long, struggling pause – as much as ten or twelve long seconds perhaps*]

HAMP It were same as I said, sir. It's same as I can't say it no different. I couldn't stand no more. I knew for sure I couldn't stand no more. I can't say it no different.

HARGREAVES Even when you were out of the battle?

HAMP It were same as it didn't matter no more where, sir. Any place I could hear guns.

HARGREAVES But God knows there's never a time when you can't hear them somewhere!

HAMP That's right, sir.

HARGREAVES Well, then, what – ?

HAMP I couldn't stand no more!

HARGREAVES But –

HAMP Lieutenant Webb, sir – 'e knew. 'E gave me extra rum.

HARGREAVES Did you say anything to him?

HAMP No, sir. Weren't nothing I could expect the like of him to do. Only what he did – giving me extra rum. But he could tell.

HARGREAVES You were in this state of mind for ten days after the attack, but you stayed put.

HAMP I knew all the time I were going to do what I did.

HARGREAVES You what?

HAMP That were another thing weren't same as any other time afore. I knew sure as death I were goin' to make tracks.

HARGREAVES You mean you planned it? You made a plan to desert and waited till the opportunity presented itself?

HAMP No, sir.

HARGREAVES But what else can I think after what you've said? Remember, I want the truth. Between you and me, the truth – plain, clean, whole truth. Please.

HAMP It weren't a plan, sir.

HARGREAVES Why did you wait for ten days?

HAMP I don't know, sir.

HARGREAVES Well, let me ask you. Let me put it this way. Surely it was because you were trying to find your courage again. You felt that you couldn't stand any more war. After all, you'd been through as much as any British soldier in France, and what you were feeling was quite natural and understandable, but you were trying, during those ten days, to regain strength to carry on.

HAMP Maybe that were right, sir. I expect it were.

HARGREAVES I want you to think about it – get it clearly into your mind. Everyone of us goes through bad times, but you didn't want to be a coward, any more than any of your comrades.

HAMP Reckon I always were, a bit, sir.

HARGREAVES So is everybody else.

HAMP But this were different.

HARGREAVES You were trying to fight off the panic that overcame you in that shell-hole.

HAMP If you speak for me, sir, you'll know better nor me what to say.

HARGREAVES But is that not the truth, or near it?

HAMP It weren't a plan, sir.

HARGREAVES Remember that – keep that clear in your mind.

medical officer HAMP I went to the M.O. that time, sir.

HARGREAVES During those ten days?

HAMP Yes, sir.

HARGREAVES Right! Now, this is important. Did you say anything to him then about your state of mind – I mean, the state of your nerves? Was that why you went to him? Who saw you, by the way?

HAMP It were Captain O'Sullivan himself, sir.

HARGREAVES And was that why you went? Did you make it clear to him?

HAMP I told him I couldn't sleep. Neither I could, sir, more'n ten minutes at once. Never like that afore. I told him.

HARGREAVES Yes? What else?

HAMP Couldn't eat much neither, sir. I told him that as well.

HARGREAVES Yes?

HAMP And I told 'im I couldn't stop shaking.

HARGREAVES That was true?

HAMP I wouldn't have said it, sir. I weren't trying anything on, sir, honest.

HARGREAVES No.

HAMP Even if I'd have thought of trying it on I wouldn't have said it to *him*, sir, if you understand me. Not Captain O'Sullivan.

HARGREAVES [With a half-smile] Yes, all right. It's just that these details are vitally important. What did Captain O'Sullivan say to you?

HAMP He give me a number nine, sir. Pills, sir. For me bowels.

HARGREAVES This was after you'd explained all these symptoms?

HAMP Yes, sir. I –

HARGREAVES Yes?

HAMP I never took it, sir.

HARGREAVES What?

HAMP The number nine. I were lucky. He weren't lookin'. I spit the pills out when he weren't lookin'. Maybe there were *some* kind o' medicine as would've helped me, sir, but, one thing I didn't have no call for was a number nine. [This with a half-embarrassed smile]

HARGREAVES Did he say anything to you – give you any advice or medical instructions?

HAMP He said I'd cold feet, sir.

HARGREAVES What else?

HAMP He said a number nine 'ud cure them.

HARGREAVES Anything else?

HAMP Can't remember no more, sir.

HARGREAVES Now I ask you to think carefully about this next question. Looking back on it, do you not believe that that interview with the M.O. must have affected your state of mind in an important way? You had gone to him for help, as you were quite entitled to do, and if you felt you had been badly let down it must have made you more confused and desperate than you were before. Was that not so?

HAMP No, sir.

HARGREAVES But surely – surely when all you got out of him was some meaningless, stupid cant about – I mean, rightly or wrongly, you must have felt badly let down.

HAMP I didn't expect any different, sir. I didn't expect him to say anythin'. Only what he told me.

HARGREAVES Why did you go, then? What did you expect?

HAMP I were only thinking, like, maybe he would give me some kind of medicine as would help me.

HARGREAVES What kind of medicine?

HAMP Well, I don't know, sir. I thought him bein' the M.O. he would know. I mean, you read about medicine in the papers at home.

HARGREAVES You mean some kind of tonic?

HAMP I forgot the name, sir.

45

HARGREAVES But that's what was in your mind? A tonic?

HAMP Aye, sir, that's what they call it. Nerve tonic, like. For my nerves. I were hoping he would think on something to help my nerves. But he never said.

HARGREAVES However, the point is that you were trying to find something that would bring your morale back.

HAMP Anything that would help me to sleep, sir, and stop me shaking and maybe, like, stop up my diarrhoea.

HARGREAVES Well, yes, all right – that's another way of saying the same thing.

HAMP Course, it wouldn't have made no difference, sir.

HARGREAVES You can't be sure of that, can you?

HAMP No, sir – only –

HARGREAVES Yes?

HAMP I knew all the time I weren't going to go back up the line. I knew I were going to make tracks, like, to get away from it.

HARGREAVES From what exactly?

HAMP Like – the guns, and –

HARGREAVES So you *had* made up your mind to desert?

HAMP No, sir. It's the God's truth I were wanting to stop myself, but it's same as I couldn't help it.

HARGREAVES You knew before you went that the battalion was going to be sent back into the line?

HAMP Yes, sir.

HARGREAVES Was that what finally decided you?

HAMP No, sir.

HARGREAVES Is that true?

HAMP Yes, sir.

HARGREAVES What did decide you, then?

HAMP There weren't nothing special, sir. Only, it were same as this night were the time for it. This night, soon as it got dark, like, I put on a bandolier, took me gas helmet and rifle – let on I had to go on a message – and I just started walking.

HARGREAVES Did you know where you were making for?

HAMP I were walking away from it, sir, that were the most of it.

HARGREAVES Had you any idea in which direction you were going?

HAMP It were the right direction.

HARGREAVES What d'you mean?

HAMP Well, I didn't get stopped. Course, I never got right away from it – not till I got on the train – but the guns were always gettin' further away. It were a daft kind of walkin', because – you'll not believe this, sir, but it's true – after I got a few miles away from the guns I got it into my head I were making for 'ome. Lamton, like. There weren't any sense in it, but it were in my head.

HARGREAVES What happened about the train?

HAMP It were stopped near a level-crossin' when I got there. Middle o' the night by that time. So I jumped on a wagon.

HARGREAVES How did you know the train was going the way you wanted to go?

HAMP I weren't sure. But it were. Coal train. Only stopped once after that. Took me a long way. I slept a while after it got daylight. No sign of guns, an' the sun shining sir. Near Calais, when I wakened up. I never knew at the time, like, but it were near Calais, and the train were slowed down, and the sun still shining. So I jumped off – and that's where they got me, the Redcaps, like, sir.

HARGREAVES What did you tell them, can you remember?

HAMP I said I were goin' on leave.

HARGREAVES Did they believe you?

HAMP No, sir.

HARGREAVES Did you expect them to?

HAMP I thought I would try it. But I didn't have no kit, and then they wanted to see me papers and then they arrested me.

HARGREAVES Did you say anything else to them – any explanation? Did you tell them about your being ill, for instance?

HAMP No, sir.

HARGREAVES Why not?

HAMP I were feeling a lot better by that time.

HARGREAVES What else did they ask you?

HAMP Nothing much.

HARGREAVES Did they say anything to you that you remember?

HAMP Only about me bein' a deserter. And I heard them saying to each other about it being a shooting job.

HARGREAVES Yes?

HAMP They'd never go that length, sir, would they? I mean shooting like. I don't think there's anybody left in A Company as 'as been out as long as me, sir. They canna shoot me.

John Wilson *Hamp*

47

Willimantic, Conn.

A company spokesman
has denied
the rumour
that all men are sailors.

He has explained
that the desert is loved
by men
and that employees
are naturally attracted to dust.
He said that clerks
were part of the caravan
of blank eyes.

As for strange dreams
of ships
and impossible fish,
he said they were a direct consequence
of wetting the lips
too often.

Lou Lipsitz

Why People Like Me are What You Would Call Bloody~Minded

Sir,—You have had a lot of letters about people being bloody minded. You have not had any that I have seen about why people like me are what you would call bloody minded.

I read your paper in the public library—I can't afford to purchase it every day. It is the same for a lot of ordinary working people like me. So you don't get much of what we think.

I am 50 years of age. I started work at 15 years of age. I will work, if I am lucky, until I am 65 years of age. I might live to 70, but I will be lucky if I can work to 70 because, even if I am able and willing, the bosses don't want us. So I shall have the old-age pension. I have not been able to save. In all my working life the money I have got will amount to about £60,000. That is the highest it could be.

don't like being without dustmen. The law of supply and demand is fine for some, but not for others. Why?

I am not a communist or an anarchist. I believe there must be differentials. But the trouble is the differentials are all wrong, and there's too much fiddling at the top. Where I work there are lavatories for bosses . . . you can only get in with a key, hot and cold, air conditioning, nice soap, individual towels. Then there are lavatories for senior staff . . hot and cold, not so good soap, a few individual towels, but good rollers. Then there is ours . . no hot and cold, rough towels, cheesecake soap. And no splash plates in the urinals. How do you think we feel about things like that in the twentieth century? Waving Union Jacks doesn't help

I saw in your paper that the Chairman of Bowring's insurance gets £57,000 a year. And of course he gets a free car, free drinks, trips abroad with his wife, etc. He gets in a year as much as I get in all my working life. The differential is a bit wrong somewhere. Or what about your reports about wills. Often you see someone, a stockbroker, for example, leaving £500,000. That is his savings, not what he lived on. It would take me 500 years to earn that little lot. Something wrong with the differential there too.

The Tory Party goes on about competition. How much competition was there when Brooke Bond put up their prices and all the others did the same. They didn't want to, they said. But they did it. Beer, petrol, milk, it all goes up the same ... what price competition?

Then we get a lot of talk about the law of supply and demand. Well, this affluent society produces a lot of effluent. So dustmen are in short supply. So they ask for more money. What a howl from the papers, T.V., radio, the lot. No howls about Brooke Bond or the others. Why? If you ask 99 people out of a hundred they can manage all right without stockbrokers. But they

It's no good economists and financial experts preaching. You can use the telly, radio, papers the lot to try to convince us that we have got to be the first to suffer. That's useless. We know the papers and the telly and radio give one side of the story. We know the other. You don't. Or you don't want to. So there will be a fight. We might lose a round or two. But we will win in the end. And if we have to fight to win instead of being sensible on both sides, the losers are going to suffer a lot.

You can call this bloody-minded. Try bringing up three kids on my pay and see how you like it. There's plenty for everybody if its shared reasonably. And if, as my mate says, we want to try to have the bridge and beaujolais as well as beer and bingo, what's wrong with that?

Yours faithfully,
JAMES THOMSON.
24 Thurrock Avenue, Aveley, Essex,
Sept. 2.

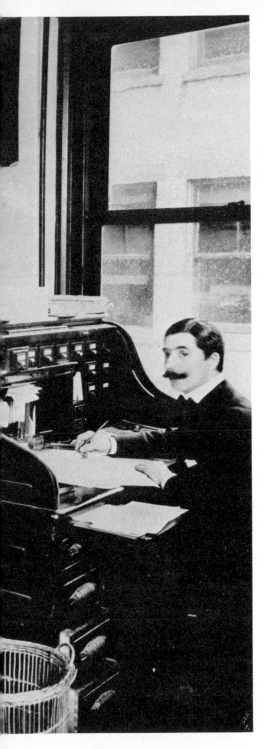

Johnny Casside, Receiving his First Pay Packet, Discovers that he has been Fined Two Shillings out of Seven and Six for 'Impudence and Disobedience'

There was Anthony, now, back from his haughty lunch, pegging away, in his clumsy manner, with his typewriter. Bony and slender as his hands were, they were slow and awkward at typing, Johnny could see that. All were back at their work, now, all busy, all but Johnny, who hung over his desk, trying to think of what to say to Anthony. He couldn't think, so he'd depend on God to put the right words into his mouth.

Several times he started for the counting-house, and several times he found himself back at the desk again, uncertain and afraid. Once he went as far as the entrance, but his heart failed him and he came back to his desk. He felt a little sick. He should have gone when he was roused, when the anger was on him.

Screw your courage to the sticking-place, said Shakespeare. 'Oh, to hell with it!' he said, roughly to himself, 'here goes!' Straightening himself stiffly, he marched to the counting-house and stood near Anthony, waiting to be noticed. After a long interval, Anthony raised his head from his typewriter and looked at Johnny.

'Well, Casside,' he said, 'what's the trouble?'

Before he could answer, the dark form and dusky face of Hewson edged its way forward from the background, and Johnny found himself loosely hemmed in between the two God-belauding brothers.

'Well,' said Anthony again, 'what is it, Casside?'

'I just came to say a word about the fine, sir.'

'All that ought to have been said has already been said,' said Anthony shortly.

Johnny conjured up all the new strength that had begun to come into his speech. He had written as many letters as he could to his brothers, trying to put into them all the things he had learned the week before, and choosing the most elegant words he could think of to describe what had happened in the locality. He had done it so well that Tom had praised him for the brightness and skill shown in the letters written to him. So with a little trembling in his mind, he settled himself down here to do what he could in his own defence.

'I don't think so, sir,' he said; 'you, yourself have said but little, and I have said nothing at all.'

'Oh!' said Anthony in an astonished voice, 'and what have you to say about it?'

Although, now and again, there was a slight quiver in it, Johnny's voice was firm and clear; and he felt that Dyke, Nearus, and the rest of them listened and were wondering.

'Well, sir,' said Johnny, 'I'd like to know, first, what was the impudence and disobedience complained of, where it happened, for which I have been fined what is, to me, a very large sum of money?'

'I see we have a lawyer amongst us!' said Hewson, with a dark grin.

'It is recent enough for you to remember it well,' said Anthony, and I've neither the time nor intention to go over it again with you. You have been fined, and there is nothing more to be said about it.'

'That's all very well, sir, but I think I have the right to say something in my own defence. The occasion that brought about what you are pleased to call disobedience and impudence was really my own time; and it was you, sir, who were unjust in keeping me beyond the stipulated hour for leaving work.'

Anthony had resumed his typing, pretending not to listen to Johnny, and there was a pause, broken by the jerky rattle of the keys clicking clumsily because of the unsteady movement of Anthony's fingers.

'Besides, sir,' went on Johnny, 'had what you allege against me happened even in the rightful time of the Firm, the amount of the fine, if you weigh it with the weekly wage I get, is altogether too large and unnecessarily severe.'

Hewson roughly pushed in past Johnny, anchoring himself beside his brother; and the two of them bent over an invoice of goods, taking as much notice of Johnny as they would of a fly on a distant star.

'I have saved up hard to buy a book I want badly,' said Johnny in a louder voice, 'and the fine had made my well-nourished plan go all agley.'

'Book!' snorted Hewson; 'maybe it's a book he wants!'

'Casside,' said Anthony, with a tinge of a smile on his bony face, 'attend to your work, and you'll have little need of books.'

'I have attended to it well,' responded Johnny vigorously, 'and for the past year not a single complaint has been made against me by a single customer. My need of books is my own need, an' that need's my own business, an' no one else's.'

'Casside,' said Hewson viciously, 'it's plain that a fine is the one thing you can understand. Go back to your work or you may have a bigger fine to face this day week!'

'I have no fear of a fine next week, for I refuse to be fined now; and what I am refusing today, I will refuse tomorrow.'

'Go back to your work, Casside,' said Anthony, a little more softly, in an effort to be kind, 'before you go too far.'

'I'll go back when the two shillings taken from me are given to me again.'

'Casside,' said Anthony solemnly, 'you will have to submit to the fine imposed upon you, or – and he paused to make what he was about to say more impressive – or leave our employment. You must make your choice.'

'I have already made it,' said Johnny.

'What is it, then?'

'To leave.'

After a moment's hesitation, Anthony opened a drawer, rooted in it, took out some silver, and flung two shillings on the desk beside Johnny.

'It is plain,' he said, 'that you are wholly unsuitable to us.'

'That's possibly something to be unashamed of,' said Johnny bitterly. 'And let me tell you there's another shilling of mine embedded in the clock you have at home! I could ill afford it. I gave it unwillingly. I thought joining in the gift would make things safer here. I need a book more'n you need a clock; but keep it; it will remind you of me when the clock strikes!'

Anthony's face went a flaming red. He bent down over his desk and remained silent. But Johnny stood there, as pale as Anthony was flushed.

'Get out!' said Hewson furiously. 'How dare you mention such a sacred thing? Get out, or get kicked out!'

Johnny sensed that the whole staff was disturbed, and he glimpsed a worried look defiling Dyke's foxy face. He had made them sit up. Whenever Anthony looked at the clock, he'd remember what Johnny had said to him.

'No one will kick me out,' said Johnny. 'I'm going. God rest you merry, gentlemen. I'm due a rest, anyway. Farewell, a long farewell to all your greatness.'

The fleshy hand of the dusky-faced Hewson sought his shoulder, giving him a push that sent Johnny colliding with the desk of Nearus.

'Get out!' he said angrily; 'this Firm has no room for a vulgar corner-boy!'

Dyke snatched the precious book from under Johnny's arm and flung it far down the passage-way into the dirty straw, a messenger meeting it with a kick that sent it away beyond into the dirtier lane.

'Follow your book,' said Dyke, 'to your rightful place in the dirt of the street!'

'There he'll find his happiness and his hope,' said Hyland. Nearus looked on and sighed and said nothing.

With his face pale as a lily lying in a dark corner, his mind a smarting hate, and rage rough in him, Johnny gathered himself together straight again, faced the two signalmen of God, saying savagely, in half a chant:

'I leave th' pair of you with your godliness and go;
And when th' ending day comes, day of wrath, I hope
You two may catch a glimpse of heaven's glory;
Then sink down, sudden, down, deep down to hell,
Amazed and sightless!'

Half blind himself with rage, he left them, picked up his precious book out of the gutter, wiped with a handkerchief the specks of cow-shit from the cover, and wended his way homewards.

Sean O'Casey *Autobiographies*

Ain't No Sense in Trying to Take Advantage

This day that I'd come up to talk was right after a big snow-storm. It was pretty cold; there was a lot of snow in the street. Traffic was moving at a snail's pace, almost at a standstill. Mama was complaining about how cold it was.

'Mama, why don't you complain to the landlord about this?'

'I called the office of the renting agency twice, and they said he wasn't in. When I called the third time, I spoke to him, but he said that it wasn't any of his problem, and I'd have to fix it up myself. I ain't got no money to be gettin' these windows relined.'

'Mama, that's a whole lot of stuff. I know better than that. Why don't you go up to the housing commission and complain about it?'

'I ain't got no time to be goin' no place complainin' about nothin'. I got all this housework to do, and all this cookin'.'

'Look, Mama, let's you and me go up there right now. I'm gonna write out a complaint, and I want you to sign it.'

'I got all this washin' to do.'

'Mama, you go on and you wash. I'm gon wait for you; I'm gon help you wash.'

Mama started washing the clothes. As soon as she finished that, she had to put the pot on the stove. Then she had to fix some lunch. As soon as she finished one thing, she would find another thing that she had to do right away. She just kept stalling for time.

Finally, after waiting for about three hours, when she couldn't find anything else to do, I said, 'Look, Mama, come on, let's you and me go out there.'

We went over to 145th Street. We were going to take the cross-town bus to Broadway, to the temporary housing-commission office.

We were waiting there. Because of the snowstorm, the buses weren't running well, so we waited there for a long time. Mama said, 'Look, we'd better wait and go some other time.'

I knew she wanted to get out of this, and I knew if I let her go and put it off to another time, it would never be done. I said, 'Mama, we can take a cab.'

'You got any money?'

'No.'

'I ain't got none either. So we better wait until another time.'

'Look, Mama, you wait right here on the corner. I'm going across the street to the pawnshop, and when I get back, we'll take a cab.'

She waited there on the corner, and I went over to the pawnshop and and pawned my ring. When I came back, we took a cab to Broadway and 145th Street, to the temporary housing-commission office. When I got there, I told one of the girls at the window that I wanted to write out a complaint against a tenement landlord.

She gave me a form to fill out and said I had to make out two copies. I sat down and started writing. It seemed like a whole lot to Mama, because Mama didn't do too much writing. She used a small sheet of paper even when she wrote a letter.

She kept bothering me while I was writing. She said, 'Boy, what's all that you puttin' down there? You can't be saying nothin' that ain't the truth. Are you sure you know what you're talking about? Because I'm only complaining about the window, now, and it don't seem like it'd take that much writing to complain about just the one window.'

'Mama, you're complaining about all the windows. Aren't all the windows in the same shape?'

'I don't know.'

'Well, look here, Mama, isn't it cold in the whole house?'

'Yeah.'

'When was the last time the windows were lined?'

'I don't know. Not since we lived in there.'

'And you been livin' there seventeen years. Look, Mama, you got to do something.'

'Okay, just don't put down anything that ain't true.' She kept pulling on my arm.

'Look, Mama, I'm gonna write out this thing. When I finish I'll let you read it, and if there's anything not true in it, I'll cross it out. Okay?'

'Okay, but it just don't seem like it take all that just to write out one complaint.'

I had to write with one hand and keep Mama from pulling on me with the other hand. When I finished it, I turned in the two complaint forms, and we left. Mama kept acting so scared, it really got on my nerves. I said, 'Look, Mama, you ain't got nothin' to be scared of.'

She said she wasn't scared, but she just wanted to stay on the good side of the landlord, because sometimes she got behind in the rent.

'Yeah, Mama, but you can't be freezin' and catching colds just because sometimes you get behind in the rent. Everybody gets behind in the rent, even people who live on Central Park West and Park Avenue. They get behind in the rent. They're not freezin' to to death just because they're behind in the rent.'

'Boy, I don't know what's wrong with you, but you're always ready to get yourself into something or start some trouble.'

'Yeah, Mama, if I'm being mistreated, I figure it's time to start some trouble.'

'Boy, I just hope to God that you don't get yourself into something one day that you can't get out of.'

'Mama, everybody grows into manhood, and you don't stop to think about that sort of thing once you become a man. You just do it, even if it's trouble that you can't get out of. You don't stop to think. Look, forget about it, Mama. Just let me worry about the whole thing.'

'Okay, you do the worryin', but the landlord ain't gon come down there in Greenwich Village and put you out. He gon put us out.'

'Mama, he ain't gon put nobody out, don't you believe me?' I pinched her on the cheek, and she got a smile out.

After a couple of days, I came back uptown. I asked Mama, 'What about the windows?'

'Nothin' about the windows.'

'What you mean "nothin' about the windows"?' I was getting a little annoyed, because she just didn't seem to want to be bothered. I said, 'You mean they didn't fix the windows yet? You didn't hear from the landlord?'

'No, I didn't hear from the landlord.'

'Well, we're going back up to the housing commission.'

'What for?'

'Because we're gon get something done about these windows.'

'But something's already been done.'

'What's been done, if you didn't hear anything from the landlord?'

'Some man came in here yesterday and asked me what windows.'

'What man?'

'I don't know what man.'

'Well, what did he say? Didn't he say where he was from?'

'No, he didn't say anything. He just knocked on the door and asked me if I had some windows that needed relining. I said, "Yeah", and he asked me what windows, so I showed him the three windows in the front.'

'Mama, you didn' show him all the others?'

'No, because that's not so bad, we didn't need them relined.'

'Mama, oh, Lord, why didn't you show him the others?'

'Ain't no sense in trying to take advantage of a good thing.'

'Yeah, Mama. I guess it was a good thing to you.'

I thought about it. I thought about the way Mama would go down to the meat market sometimes, and the man would sell her some meat that was spoiled, some old neck bones or some pig tails. Things that weren't too good even when they weren't spoiled. And sometimes she would say, 'Oh, those things aren't too bad.' She was scared to take them back, scared to complain until somebody said, 'That tastes bad.' Then she'd go down there crying and mad at him, wanting to curse the man out. She had all that Southern upbringing in her, that business of being scared of Mr Charlie. Everybody white she saw was Mr Charlie.

Claude Brown _Manchild in the Promised Land_

A Plea to White Men to Join the March on Washington, 28 August 1963

At nightfall
there is a soft knocking
on the doors –

the great wooden doors,
hammered shut
and sealed
all these years –

And outside
there are shouts, faces,
cities and lonely roads.
Millions of people
are alive
and go from house to house
knocking on the doors.

Outside
men's hopes
hold out their hands to you –
worn hands, with blackness in the folds
of the knuckles;
with great nails, smashed and disfigured
as if hit with a hammer.

Where are you?

Lou Lipsitz

Song of the Rice Bargees

In the town up river
We'll get a mouthful of rice,
But the barge we're hauling is heavy,
And the water flows downward.
We'll never arrive up there.

Pull faster, mouths
Are waiting for food.
Pull together, don't jostle
The man beside.

Soon night will come. The camp,
Too small for a dog's shadow,
Costs a mouthful of rice.
The shore is so slippery
We can't move an inch.

Pull faster, mouths
Are waiting for food.
Pull together, don't jostle
The man beside.

The rope that cuts
Our shoulders lasts longer than us.
The overseer's whip
Has seen four generations.
When will it see the last?

Pull faster, mouths
Are waiting for food.
Pull together, don't jostle
The man beside.

Our fathers pulled the barge from the rivermouth
Up stream a little further. Our children
Will reach the source. We
Come between.

Pull faster, mouths
Are waiting for food.
Pull together, don't jostle
The man beside.

There's rice in the barge. The farmer who
Picked it was given
A handful of coin, we
Get still less. An ox would cost
More. There's too many of us.

Pull faster, mouths
Are waiting for food.
Pull together, don't jostle
The man beside.

When the rice reaches the town
And the children ask who
Dragged the heavy barge they're told:
It was just dragged.

Pull faster, mouths
Are waiting for food.
Pull together, don't jostle
The man beside.

The food from below comes
To the feeders above. Those
Who haul it up, they
Have not eaten.

Bertolt Brecht
Translated from the German by
Christopher Middleton

The Pueblo

That man I remember well, and at least two centuries
have passed since I saw him;
he travelled neither on horseback nor in a carriage –
purely on foot
he undid
the distances,
carrying neither sword nor weapon
but nets on his shoulder,
axe or hammer or spade;
he never fought with another of his kind –
his struggle was with water or with earth,
with the wheat, for it to become bread,
with the towering tree, for it to yield wood,
with the walls, to open doors in them,
with the sand, constructing walls,
and with the sea, to make it bear fruit.

I knew him and still he is there in me.

The carriages splintered in pieces,
war destroyed doorways and walls,
the city was a fistful of ashes,
all the dresses withered into dust,
and he persists, for my sake,
he survives in the sand,
where everything previously
seemed durable except him.

In the comings and goings of families,
at times he was my father or my relative
or (it may have been, it may not)
perhaps the one who did not come home
because water or earth devoured him
or a machine or a tree killed him,
or he was that funeral carpenter
who walked behind the coffin, but dry-eyed,
someone who never had a name
except as wood or metal have,
and on whom others looked from above,
unable to see
the ant for the ant-hill;
so that when his feet no longer moved
because, poor and tired, he had died,
they never saw what they were not used to seeing –
already other feet walked in his place.

The other feet were still him,
equally the other hands,
the man persisted –
when it seemed that now he was spent,
he was the same man over again,
there he was once more, tilling the soil,
cutting cloth, but without a shirt,
there he was and was not, as before,
he had gone and was back again,
and since he never had cemetery
nor tomb, nor his name engraved
on the stone that he sweated to cut,
nobody ever knew of his arrival
and nobody knew when he died,
thus only when the poor man was able
did he come back to life again, unnoticed.

He was the man all right, without inheritance,
cattle or coat of arms,
and he did not stand out from the others,
the others who were himself,
from above he was grey like clay,
he was drab as leather,
he was yellow harvesting wheat,
he was black deep in the mine,
he was stone-coloured in the castle,
in the fishing boat, the colour of tunny,
horse-coloured in the meadow –
how could anyone distinguish him
if they were inseparable, the element,
earth, coal or sea, in the guise of a man?

Where he lived, everything
a man touched would grow:
the hostile stones,
hewn
by his hands,
took shape and form
and one by one took on
the sharp clarity of buildings,
he made bread with his hands,
set the trains running,
the distances bred townships,
other men grew up,
the bees arrived,
and through man's creating and multiplying,
spring wandered into the market place
between doves and bakeries.

The father of the loaves was forgotten,
he who cut and walked, beating
and opening paths, shifting sand,
when everything else existed, he existed no longer,
he gave away his existence, that was everything.
He went somewhere else to work and ultimately
he went into death, rolling
like a river stone –
death carried him off downstream.

I, who knew him, saw him go down
till he existed only in what he was leaving –
streets he could scarcely be aware of
houses he never never would inhabit.

I come back to see him, and every day I wait.

I see him in his coffin and resurrected.

I pick him out from all
the others who are his equals
and it seems to me that it cannot be,
that in this way, we are going nowhere,
to survive so has no glory.

I believe that Heaven must include
that man, properly shod and crowned.

I think that those who made so many things
ought to be masters of everything.

And those who make bread ought to eat!

And those in the mine should have light!

Enough by now of grey men in chains!

Enough of the pale lost ones!

Not another man will go past except as a ruler.

Not a single woman without her diadem.

Gloves of gold for every hand.

Fruits of the sun for all the obscure ones!

I knew that man, and when I could,
when he still had eyes in his head,
when he still had a voice in his throat,
I sought him among the tombs, and I said to him,
pressing his arm that was still not dust:

'Everything will pass, and you will still be living.

You set fire to life.

You made what is yours.'

So let no one worry when
I seem to be alone and am not alone,
I am not with nobody and I speak for all —

Someone is listening to me and, although they do not know it,
those I sing of, those who know
go on being born and will fill up the world.

Pablo Neruda *Translated from the Spanish by Robert Bly*

Red-Indian View of Education

At the treaty of Lancaster, in Pennsylvania, anno 1744, between the Government of Virginia and the Six Nations, the commissioners from Virginia acquainted the Indians by a speech, that there was at Williamsburg a college with a fund for educating Indian youth; and that if the chiefs of the Six Nations would send down half a dozen of their sons to that college, the government would take care that they be well provided for, and instructed in all the learning of the white people.

The Indians' spokesman replied:

'We know that you highly esteem the kind of learning taught in those colleges, and that the maintenance of our young men, while with you, would be very expensive to you. We are convinced, therefore, that you mean to do us good by your proposal and we thank you heartily.

'But you, who are wise, must know that different nations have different conceptions of things; and you will not therefore take it amiss, if our ideas of this kind of education happen not to be the same with yours. We have had some experience of it; several of our young people were formerly brought up at the colleges of the northern provinces; they were instructed in all your sciences; but, when they came back to us, they were bad runners, ignorant of every means of living in the woods, unable to bear either cold or hunger, knew neither how to build a cabin, take a deer, nor kill an enemy, spoke our language imperfectly, were therefore neither fit for hunters, warriors nor counsellors; they were totally good for nothing.

'We are, however, not the less obligated by your kind offer, though we decline accepting it, and to show our grateful sense of it, if the gentlemen in Virginia will send us a dozen of their sons, we will take care of their education, instruct them in all we know, and make men of them.'

Benjamin Franklin

The Destruction of the Red Indian

All the Indian tribes who once inhabited the territory of New England – the Narragansetts, the Mohicans, the Pequots – now live only in men's memories; the Lenapes, who received Penn one hundred and fifty years ago on the banks of the Delaware, have now vanished. I have met the last of the Iroquois; they were begging. All of the nations I have just named once reached to the shores of the ocean; now one must go more than a hundred leagues inland to meet an Indian. These savages have not just drawn back, they have been destroyed. As the Indians have withdrawn and died, an immense nation is taking their place and constantly growing. Never has such a prodigious development been seen among the nations, nor a destruction so rapid. . . .

At the end of the year 1831 I was on the left bank of the Mississippi, at the place the Europeans call Memphis. While I was there a numerous band of Choctaws (or Chactas as they are called by the French of Louisiana) arrived; these savages were leaving their country and seeking to pass over to the right bank of the Mississippi, where they hoped to find an asylum promised to them by the American government. It was then the depths of winter, and that year the cold was exceptionally severe; the snow was hard on the ground, and huge masses of ice drifted on the river. The Indians brought their families with them; there were among them the wounded, the sick, newborn babies and old men on the point of death. They had neither tents nor wagons, but only some provisions and weapons. I saw them embark to cross the great river, and the sight will never fade from my memory. Neither sob nor complaint rose from that silent assembly. Their afflictions were of long standing, and they felt them to be irremediable. All the Indians had already got into the boat that was to carry them across; their dogs were still on the bank; as soon as the animals finally realized that they were being left behind for ever, they all together raised a terrible howl and plunged into the icy waters of the Mississippi to swim after their masters.

Alexis de Tocqueville *Democracy in America (first published 1835)*

From a Letter to a Teacher

Dear Miss

You won't remember me or my name. You have failed so many of us.

On the other hand I have often had thoughts about you, and the other teachers, and about that institution which you call 'school' and about the boys that you fail.

You fail us right out into the fields and factories and there you forget us.

While giving a test you used to walk up and down between the rows of desks and see me in trouble and making mistakes, but you never said a word.

I have the same situation at home. No one to turn to for help for miles around. No books. No telephone.

Now here I am 'in school'. I came from far away to be taught. Here I don't have to deal with my mother, who promised to be quiet and then interrupted me a hundred times. My sister's little boy is not here to ask me for help with his homework. Here I have silence and good light and a desk all to myself.

And over there, a few steps away, you stand. You know all of these things. You are paid to help me.

Instead, you waste your time keeping me under guard as if I were a thief.

You know even less about men than we do. The lift serves as a good machine for ignoring the people in your building; the car, for ignoring people who travel in buses; the telephone for avoiding seeing people's faces or entering their homes.

Cicero: a Latin writer   I don't know about you, but your students who know Cicero* – how many families of living men do they know intimately? How many of their kitchens have they visited? How many of their sick have they sat with through the night? How many of their dead have they borne on their shoulders? How many can they trust when they are in distress? . . .

A thousand motors roar under your windows every day. You have no idea to whom they belong or where they are going.

But I can read the sounds of my valley for miles around. The sound of the motor in the distance in Nevio going to the station, a little late. If you like, I can tell you everything about hundreds of people, dozens of families and their relatives and personal ties.

hill farmer   Whenever you speak to a worker you manage to get it all wrong: your choice of words, your tone, your jokes. I can tell what a mountaineer is thinking even when he keeps silent, and I know what's on his mind even when he talks about something else.

This is the sort of culture your poets should have given you. It is the culture of nine-tenths of the earth, but no one has yet managed to put it down in words or pictures or films.

Be a bit humble, at least. Your culture has gaps as wide as ours. Perhaps even wider. Certainly more damaging to a teacher in the elementary schools.

At the gymnastics exam the teacher threw us a ball and said, 'Play basketball.' We didn't know how. The teacher looked us over with contempt: 'My poor children.'

He, too, is one of you. The ability to handle a conventional ritual seemed so vital to him. He told the principal that we had not been given any 'physical education' and we should take the exams again in the autumn.

Any one of us could climb an oak tree. Once up there we could let go with our hands and chop off a two-hundred pound branch with a hatchet. Then we could drag it through the snow to our mother's doorstep.

I heard of a gentleman in Florence who rides upstairs in his house in a lift. But then he has bought himself an expensive gadget and pretends to row in it. You would give him an A in physical education.

The School of Barbiana *Translated from the Italian by Nora Rossi and Tom Cole*

Escape from School

Mr Seaton was a new master who'd become devoted to Old Kip's ideas, and had even invented a new variety of moral responsibility. He was the mathematics master, and his new invention was that you marked your own maths papers according to a complicated system which I never understood. At the end of the week he asked you what your marks were, and you told him on your 'Scout's honour'. I never had the remotest idea what my marks were and I used to award myself a figure I hoped would be low enough not to attract attention,

and high enough to keep me out of trouble. But one morning I had the misfortune to be asked first, and I said 85, glibly enough, and then realized in the silence that that was very high indeed. So I said, 'Oh – no sir, I mean 35,' and I peered at my exercise to make it appear that I'd mistaken a three for an eight. Mr Seaton came striding up and, of course, was unable to find evidence of either figure, among the muddled miseries of my calculations. So he began to shout. 'Stand up, boy. Admit, boy, you have no idea. Does your Scout's honour mean nothing to you? Are you prepared to cheat and lie your way through life?' He went on and on and finally barked out: 'I shall inform the headmaster that I've a cheat in my form.'

It was the last lesson in the afternoon of a perfect July day. Mr Seaton, I knew, would inform the headmaster at dinner that night. The school would be summoned after lunch the next day. Meanwhile there was an hour's free time before tea. The heavy sweet smell of the country drifted in through the elm avenue where the rooks were cawing away like mad, the classroom was dusty, ink-stained, and suddenly very narrow and confining like a jail. Outside you could hear the country breathing sleepily and calmly in the sunshine. I made up my mind. I'd go – now. And with that decision, all in a second, I was as happy as Larry. I went out onto the lawn, and stood on top of the north bank among the trees for a minute or two looking around. And then I slipped through the elm avenue, under the cawing rooks, over the wall, over the road, and onto the field path which led winding up and down a thick green slope, to the field of white stones which was the limit of my explorations on Sunday walks.

For the rest of that summer evening I loafed through the sweet grass, and the long ditches full of ragged-robin, where the cow parsley was up to my waist, entirely at one with the universe: I sucked grasses, climbed trees, avoided villages, paddled in streams, and finally, when it began to grow dark, I found a cow shed, in a paddled patch of sun-baked mud in a thread-bare field on a western slope, and lay down in some old-smelling hay inside, and went to sleep. That mood was still with me in the morning. A wonderful morning with the sun sparkling all new on everything, and a soft wind and a glittering green downward slope to start my journey with, and in this delightful world, there was no washing.

But now I was getting near Leicester, and the villages grew more and more frequent and soon they were continuous. I was very tired, and going very slowly. A cold wind blew up and though I tried hard to skirt Leicester and get out into the country again, I only half succeeded, and spent most of the day bitterly among the tramlines. Clouds covered the sky. At about seven o'clock that evening, clogged with fatigue, I was plodding along a black road, through rows of ugly miners' cottages in a cold rain. I'd nothing left but obstinacy. And about a mile out of Desford on the north road towards Ashby, a bicycle came suddenly up from behind me and stopped, barring my way. It was an enormous fat scarlet policeman, with a heavy old-Bill moustache. 'Where y' going lad,' he said, beaming at me through the rain. 'I'm just walkin',' I said. 'Ah, walkin' are you?' He looked me up and down. 'Well, what about a bite to eat?' 'Yes,' I said, 'I could do with that.' 'Then us'll just tek a little walk back and fix it up,' he said. We walked back to a miner's cottage of blackened red brick, and there was his wife, if possible redder and larger than he was. A huge fire, what they call a collier's fire in those parts, filled the grate and half the chimney. It was as hot as the tropics, and what small space was left in the room when these enormous figures sat down was filled with china dogs, bowls of plants, shepherdesses and pictures of virgins locked out in the snow.

There was a fat cat, and a proper black kettle singing on the hob. They stuffed me with bacon and eggs, and bread and butter and jam, and enough tea to float a battleship. They laughed all the time. 'Eat up, lad. That's right. Never let 'em get you down,' said the policeman. 'And how are you, eh? Fit as a fiddle, eh? Now I suppose your name – it couldn't be Cutforth, could it?' 'Yes, it is,' I said. 'Well, you've done a fair walk,' he said. 'How did you like it?' I said that up till today I'd never liked anything better. 'That's the stuff, lad. Well, I'll just go and do a bit of telephoning, and I'll be back.' When he came back he said, 'Now, how did you come to start this bit of a walk, like?' I thought he was a very sensible man. He appeared to have no moral responsibility of any kind. So I told him the whole story, with an imitation of Old Kip holding forth about the 'disapproval of his fellows'. The policeman and his wife rocked to and fro beating their sides in an ecstasy of laughter. 'Nay,' the policeman said. 'Nay, it sounds a proper rum auction, that school. And that Kip, he's a proper comic cut.' Now this was to me an entirely new idea. It had never occurred to me that it was possible to criticize the set-up. Actually to think of the school in that lordly way as a 'rum auction' and Old Kip as a 'proper comic cut' – it was a new and welcome outlook.

'I can see,' the policeman went on, 'as you'd no other course, but to
whiner get out and keep cheerful. I never could abide a whinger. A whinging kid I cannot stomach. Your dad – I've just rung him on the phone, and he'll be here directly. Your dad, I suppose, being a gentleman, won't have the guts – er – to give that young master a bloody nose same as I would. But take my advice, lad – you go back to that school, and face 'em out, and never let 'em get you down.' My father arrived in the car shortly afterwards, and my new friend immediately changed into a comic turn himself, touching his forelock and saying 'Here's my best respects,' and being tipped very heavily.

It was decided that I should go back, and two or three days later my father left me in Old Kip's study. He said, 'So you have decided to return. I think that is a wise decision. The boys have been prepared for your reappearance among them. I think an attitude of bravado will not go down at all well. You will receive no punishment. But I wish you to realize some part of the great anxiety of which you have been the cause. There is just one thing: your behaviour has caused grave sorrow to Mr Seaton, and he's waiting in the next room to receive your apology should you wish to give it. But I leave it to you. It is your own moral responsibility. Shall I tell him to come in?' I took a deep breath and shouldered my moral responsibility. 'No, sir,' I said. And went in to tea to face the school.

René Cutforth *Order to View*

A Beating

Without his usual cut of bread for lunch that day Johnny sat on a
mangy clump of grass watching, with his good eye, Georgie
Middleton and a group of cronies sitting between two church
buttresses, playing cards, smoking fags and arguing vigorously.
He looked, came nearer; and Middleton lifted his head, and smiled.

'Come over here, and stand near me for luck,' he said to Johnny.

Johnny came nearer, a little shyly, leaned a hand on Georgie's
shoulder, and watched the play. They were playing twenty-fives
for a penny a game and a ha'penny for the best trump out each deal.
After every sixth game a boy took his turn for the following six
games to stand aside and keep watch in case they should be suddenly
surprised by oul' Slogan coming upon them unawares. Massey was
now watching, and impatiently waiting for the six games to pass so
that he could get back to the sport again. The cards were dealt, the
tricks played and gathered, and Middleton won. Again the cards
were dealt, given out, the tricks played and gathered, and again
Middleton won.

'That's the third game for me, hand-runnin',' said Middleton
delightedly. 'Look alive, Ecret, and deal while the luck's my way.'

'I'll deal,' ejaculated Massey. 'That's the sixth game, now, and it's
Ecret's turn to stand and keep nix.'

'It's only the fifth,' responded Ecret, 'there's another game to go yet.'

'Sixth, I tell you,' persisted Massey; 'didn't I count them carefully?
So up with you off your hunkers, and take my place here.'

'I tell you it's only the fifth game,' growled Ecret, as he shuffled the card:

'Sixth, sixth, sixth,' repeated Massey impatiently, and he stretched
over to take the pack of cards from Ecret's hands.

'No blasted bickerin', now, while I'm winnin',' said Middleton testily.

'But fair's fair,' grumbled Massey. 'I've watched here through the
six games; and accordin' to rules, it's Ecret's turn to take my place
and keep nix for the crowd.'

'Sit down then,' snapped Middleton, eager to get another penny in
the pool while he was winning; 'sit down, if you want a hand so
badly, and Johnny, here, will keep nix for us all.' He looked up at
Johnny, and added, 'Make yourself useful, Johnny, be keepin' your
good eye well peeled, an' if you see oul' balls Slogan turning the
corner, give us the tip so that we'll all be talkin' about David
watchin' Bathsheba havin' her bath, before he comes close.'

Johnny became almost ill with fear that he wouldn't see Slogan
quick enough, if he came round the corner. He hadn't the courage to
say that his eye wasn't good enough; so he strained this one eye open,

and stared fixedly at the corner round which Slogan would probably come, if he came at all. He prayed that he would not come, and that the bell would shortly be heard proclaiming that the time for cards was past, and that all must return to the song of the spelling and the sums.

'Somebody shy in the pool,' said Middleton; 'only ninepence in it, so there's a wing missin' – who's shy?'

'I am,' said Massey, who was dealing the cards. When he had given them out, he added a penny to the pool. 'Ecret's lead, and spades is trumps,' he added, peering expectantly into his hand.

They led and trumped and took their tricks; shuffled and cut and led and trumped and took their tricks, while Johnny stared and stared at the corner round which danger might come, and longed and longed for the warning bell to ring.

Suddenly there shot into his eyes a pain like the piercing of many needles, flooding into an agony that shocked his brain and flashed a glare of crimson light before him that made him clench his teeth and press his lids tight together till a stream of scalding evil tears forced their way between them, and ran hotly down his cheeks. Then he felt himself jerked back by the shoulders, and heard the sound of scrambling feet. When the pain subsided, he opened the good eye, and saw Slogan taking up the money in the pool, and gathering the cards, with a scowl on his face; while the group of boys looked on, embarrassed and silent. When Slogan had gathered up all the money and the cards, without speaking a word, he left them standing there, awkward and resentful.

Middleton turned savagely on Johnny.

'How the hell did you manage to let him sail down on the top of us like that?' he snarled, but Johnny, burning with shame and shaking with sensitive fear, gave out no answer.

'Caught us all, like a lot of shaggy sheep,' muttered Massey.

Middleton turned and struck Johnny sharply across the mouth with the back of his hand, making the boy's lip bleed, as he shouted, 'You half-blind, sappy-lidded, dead-in-the-head dummy, you couldn't keep your eyes skinned for a minute or two an' save the few bob we were bettin' from buyin' Bibles for the heathen buggers of Bengal!'

'Caught us all, like a lot of shaggy sheep,' muttered Massey.

Middleton gave Johnny a vicious shove that sent him reeling.

'Away, for Christ's sake outa me sight, you hand-gropin' pig's-eye-in-a-bottle, you!'

The others laughed, crowded round Johnny, pushed and pinched him, as he turned and walked slowly away from them.

Turning the corner, he heard Slogan belling the end of the play-hour; and, passing the master, he entered the schoolroom, sat down in his place, and screwed his good eye into a lesson book, while his heart thumped in his breast. The boys poured into the school, and his classmates sat down beside him, whispering excitedly about all that had happened.

Suddenly the hum of the school was hushed, for Slogan, standing at his desk at the upper end of the room, was ringing his bell, and all the boys, save Johnny, knew that when the bell was rung from that place some very important thing was about to be said by the master. All that were in the school heard the master's voice coming out of the stillness, with a dull tone of joy in it, like the quavering notes of a sickening bird.

'As I was walking about the playground today – prowling about, I think you all call it – I caught a number of our more respectable boys deep in a very sinful pastime, a pastime that we can safely associate only with papist corner-boys; to wit too-whoo videlicet, card-playing, and gambling like good ones in this game with the devil's prayer book, forgetful that they were protestant boys baptized in the brine of the Boyne water giving them a greater responsibility to behave blameless before God and man and roman catholics, who are always on the alert to exaggerate any little indiscretion that respectable protestant boys may commit. In the first feeling of righteous indignation that came over me, I was going to make an example of every boy connected with this sin by giving each a sound and thorough whaling; but instead of that, I will leave it to their conscience to punish them more than a firm application of the cane could. But there is a certain boy mixed up with it whom no one would think, at first go, could be connected with the card-gambling, and this boy must be punished; and I am going to punish this boy now, and punish him well. I am going to punish him in such a way that he will think twice before he indulges in the vice again. This brave little fellow, on whom I'm going to test the valour of my cane, was on the *qui vive* so that the card-school wouldn't be disturbed by the bold bad teacher, but this brave little boy didn't watch well enough. He fell asleep at his post, and in a few minutes he is going to feel very sorry that he didn't keep a better Spartan watch and ward. That little boy's mother is a widow, so he has no father to take care of him; and it is meet, right, and my bounden duty to do everything possible to make sure that no bad tendencies are allowed to creep into the nature of the widow's little son. And when I have reddened his backside with this cane, I'm sure he'll be a better and more careful little boy for a long time to come, and run a mile away from a card whenever he sees one.' He swished the cane through the air, and grinningly asked the school, 'Who was he who said, spare the rod and spoil the child, boys?'

'Solomon, sir Solomon, sir,' shouted a dozen of the boys.

'And in what part of the Bible do we read that counsel?'

'Proverbs, chapter thirteen, verse twenty-four,' shouted a dozen of the boys.

'And what are the exact words, boys?'

There was a dead silence, and only one boy held up his hand.

'Well, Ecret, my boy, tell the dunces the exact words used by the wise man, Solomon, when he advises us to deal in a bright way with bold boys.'

'He that spareth his rod hateth his son,' sang out Ecret, with his head up.

'And wasn't Solomon inspired of God?' asked Slogan.

'Yessir,' responded the school.

'How do we prove that?' questioned the master.

The school was silent.

'All Holy Scripture is inspired of God,' said Slogan, 'and the Book of Proverbs is part of Holy Scripture, and chapter thirteen and verse twenty-four is part of the Book of Proverbs; *ergo*, the counsel in the verse, he that spareth his rod hateth his son, is holy and inspired of God without a possible doubt. So, boys, wouldn't it be very sinful of me to neglect or despise the teaching inspired of God, seeing that I stand *in loco parentis* to you all, and particularly to the widow's little son, brave little Johnny Casside?'

'Yessir, Yessir,' responded the whole school, all save only Georgie Middleton, for Johnny saw that his head hung down, and that he took no part in what was going on between the boys and their master.

'The ayes have it,' said Slogan, nodding brightly towards the boys; 'so come along, Johnny, come along up here to me, my son, till I pay you the attention counselled of God, which will be painful, but which will, ultimately, add a lot to your moral and, I hope, spiritual progress.'

'Slogan's callin' y'up,' whispered a boy on Johnny's right; 'wants to biff you for playin' cards durin' playhour, so he does.' But Johnny cowered his head down to the desk, and made no offer to stir.

'Eh, there,' said a boy to his left, nudging him in the side, 'd'ye hear? He's callin' you. Y'are to g'up to him – d'ye hear?'

'Come along, boy,' said Slogan, down to Johnny; 'come along, and get it over.' But Johnny hung his head towards the desk, and made no offer to stir.

'He hesitates,' said Slogan. 'Thus conscience doth make cowards of us all; and thus the native hue of resolution is sicklied o'er with the pale cast of thought. Come on, come up here.'

'He's not makin' a single move to stir sir,' said the boy on Johnny's left.

'Come on, come up, come up, come on,' chirruped the master. 'Remember what your godfathers and godmothers promised for you – to submit yourself lowly and reverently to all your governors, teachers, spiritual pastors and masters; so up you come; and in later years you'll rejoice when you remember the caning a good master gave you.' Then he looked down at Johnny, and went on in a voice of quiet and steady sternness: 'Are you going to come up quietly, boy, to take your medicine, or must I go down, and wallop you up to me?'

Johnny slowly and fearfully climbed out of the desk, and taking as many steps as possible, came towards Slogan, his heart thumping hard, and the sweat breaking out all over his forehead. He felt that Slogan wanted to beat away on him the fear that made him afraid to lay a hand on the other and bigger boys; for he had heard Middleton, Massey and Ecret say that if Slogan ever tried any thrick of caning them, they'd open his bald skull with a slate. He halted a little distance away from the master, just out of reach of the cane.
'A little nearer, a little nearer, boy,' purred Slogan; 'you've got to get it, so make up your mind to take it like a little Spartan. Tell me, boy, what's a Spartan? He doesn't know what a Spartan is,' grinned Slogan, turning towards the school. 'Well, Spartans lived a long time ago in Greece, and were famous for bearing pain without a murmur. In Sparta every little boy, whether good or bad, was continually caned to make him hardy. So just shut your mouth, close your eyes, take your caning calmly, and all the school will look upon you as a little Spartan. I see your britches are a little threadbare, but that will make it all the more exciting for you. Now all we want are two strong and willing boys to come up here and stand ready to hold you down, if you squirm too much, so that you can get the full benefit of a kindly, if stern, Christian castigation. Whom shall I choose for the honour?' And Slogan looked slowly and lovingly at the tense figures sitting in bunched-up lines in the yellow wooden desks.

'Will I do, sir?' called out Massey, popping up his hand to attract the master's attention.

'You, Massey,' said the master, 'will do nicely for one. You're pretty strong; and, if the need arises, I'm sure you will do your duty. Now, just one more. The biggest boy in the school ought to have the honour of holding the boy down – you, Georgie, come along here, and help.'

Middleton's face reddened as he bent his head down to the desk and muttered, 'I'd rather not, sir.'

Slogan put a hand behind a less-deaf ear, bent forward sideways, and said, 'Eh?'

Middleton, keeping his head bent, raised his voice and said doggedly,

'I'd rather not, sir. I want no hand in any boy's batterin''; an' besides, the kid's too delicate to touch.'

Slogan went white to the gills.

'Middleton,' he said, with quiet bitterness, 'you had better learn to give an opinion only when your master asks for one.'

Middleton suddenly stood up, and a dirty, dog-like scowl lined his harsh face as he pressed his soiled hands on the top of the desk so hard that the knuckles whitened.

'The kid had nothing to do with it,' he rasped out; 'it was me and the others. He didn' play, an' doesn't know how, an' he kep' nix because we made him.'

A deep silence spread over the whole school.

'Georgie Middleton,' said Slogan, in a dead level voice, glancing over the whole school with his shallow eyes, 'will be leaving us all in a month or two to go out and fight his way in the world, and I'm sure we all wish him the best of luck. He is to try for a job in a big store where the manager wishes to give a start to a boy who has just left school. Mr Middleton has asked our rector to give Georgie a character, and the rector has asked me for a general report of his conduct here. If Georgie wants to get on in the world with the help of a good start, I'd advise him to be careful to make his master think well of him. Am I right, Georgie Middleton?' asked Slogan, now fixing his eyes on the head-bent boy.

Middleton fought his fear for a moment, then the whole school heard him murmur, 'Yessir,' as he sank into his seat, shocked into the feeling that dangers flooded the way of an open courage.

'And don't you think, Georgie, that this boy here should be punished for his own sake?' went on the master. There was a pause, and then the whole school heard the murmur of Yessir from the mouth of Middleton.

'Come along up here, then,' said Slogan, 'and stand ready to help as soon as I need you.' And Middleton, pale, and a little sick with shame, slouched up; and, sullen and bitter-minded, stood near the radiant, iron-bowelled, ratty-hearted master, who put his hand out and patted Georgie's shoulder.

'You're a good boy, Georgie,' he said, 'for you have had the manliness to acknowledge an error which many of us might very well hesitate to do; and there is more joy in heaven over one sinner that repenteth than over ninety and nine that need no repentance. And now,' he went on, gripping Johnny by the collar of his coat, 'we start to cane a little conscience and a lot of caution into the soul of a wilful little boy.'

Johnny shook when he felt the grip on his shoulder, and his stomach went a little sick with the foreknowledge of the pain that was to come upon him.

'Me mother said I wasn't to be touched because me eyes are bad,' he said hurriedly and imploringly. 'Don't beat me, and I'll promise I'll never do the like again.' Then he felt the searing sting of the cane across his thighs, and he screamed and tore at the master with his little hands, twisted his body and lashed out with his feet at the master's shins. Some of the kicks got home, the master gave a dog's yelp, and a burning glare of cruelty shot into his paly eyes.

'Here, Massey, and you, Middleton,' he yelled, 'hold his arms stretched out over the desk till I knock the devil of resistance out of him!'

The two boys caught hold of Johnny's arms and pulled him over the desk, leaving him at the mercy of the smiter, while the panting boy pleaded, 'Please, sir, don't. I didn't mean to watch for the card-playin', really I didn' – oh, you're cuttin' the skin off me!'

But the bastard, sweating and puffing, with rigid snarling face and shining eyes, panted and sliced and cut and cut again and again. Johnny felt Massey twisting his arm, pretending that he was hard to hold. Slogan, at last easing off, gave a few more vicious strokes, then stopped to wipe his face in his handkerchief.

'Up on the chair with you, now, beside the desk,' he said to the quivering boy, 'and let the school have a good look at you.' A slice across the legs sent Johnny, with a suppressed cry, to leap quick on to the chair, chorused by a titter from the school at his haste to get there. Ashamed to rub the maddening sting in his backside and legs before the school, he balanced himself on the chair, with the eye-bandage that had loosened in the struggle, hanging round his neck, his eyes torturing him with the ache of the disease and the tears that had poured out of them, and his whole nature shaken with the confused wonder at what people were doing to him and what people were thinking of him; there he stood balancing on the chair, doing his best to check the sobs that tossed about the very beating of his heart.

Slogan looked at him for a minute, and then shook his head, and there was contempt in the shake.

'He wasn't much of a Spartan, after all,' he said, turning to the school, with a grin, 'and the opinion I have of him now is less than the one I had before. Well, we'll have to be careful of him, for one sickly sheep infects the flock, and poisons all the rest.' He glanced again at Johnny. 'We'll give him a minute or two to pull himself together and try to be a man, but if he goes on annoying the school with his baby blubbering, we'll have to cane him quiet – isn't that so?'

'Yessir,' chorused the school.

A bell rang for change of positions; those who had been seated in desks, formed into standing classes, and those who had been standing, sat themselves down in the desks. Johnny still shook a little with gentle crying till Slogan stood before him, angry, threatening, cane in hand.

'Finish the whinging, finish the whinging, boy, quick, or' – and he shook the arm of Johnny. The boy tried to check the sobbing, tried to look calm, and sobbed again.

'Stop it at once. D'ye hear? Are you finished?'

'Yessir,' murmured Johnny.

'Finished, quite, quite finished, are you?'

'Yessir.'

'Well, let's hear no more of it. Not a squeak out of you, or the cane'll be twisting round your legs again.'

With a steady effort of will, Johnny kept quiet, stood sullen on the chair, and waited and watched Slogan return to his desk, and bend over it to correct exercises. He looked at the thin stream of sunlight flowing in by the door, left open to give air to a room hot with the breath of children and teacher.

Then the bell rang again, and all that were standing filed into the desks. The Regulations of the Board of Education were turned with their face to the wall, and an oblong strip of millboard having written on it, Religious Education, was turned to face the school. Rapping on his desk with a heavy, glossy ebony ruler, Slogan silenced the murmur of the school. He put down the ruler on the desk beside him, and bent his hoary oul' head, saying softly, 'Let us pray.'

There was a clatter of moving bodies as all got down on to their knees. Slogan knelt down, too, resting his hoary oul' head on his arms that rested on the seat of the chair from which he had risen to pray. The ebony ruler lay motionless on the desk beside him.

'O Lord, open Thou our eyes that we may behold wonderful things out of Thy law.' The ebony ruler lay quiet on the desk beside him. 'Our Father which art in heaven. Hallowed by Thy Name.' Johnny could see the pink baldy head of him, with its hoary edging, as Slogan bent down over the seat of the chair on which his arms rested.

Johnny suddenly slipped down from the chair he stood on, a flood of mighty rage swept through him; he whipped up the heavy ebony ruler, and with all the hate in all his heart, in all his mind, in all his soul, and in all his strength, and a swift upward swing of his arm, he brought the ebony ruler down on the pink, baldy, hoary oul' head of hoary oul' Slogan, feeling a desperate throb of joy when he heard the agonizing yell that Slogan let out of him when the ebony ruler fell.

Still gripping the ebony ruler, he made for the open door and the sun. He saw Georgie Middleton grip Ecret's shoulder as Ecret made a movement to rise and stop his flight. He saw, as he flew past, the hand of Massey stretched out to hinder, and he heard the blasting curse of Massey in his ears as the ebony ruler came down on the outstretched hand. Away out through the door he dashed, across the road, down the narrow mucky Brady's Lane, shinned speedily up the rough-cut stone wall of the railway embankment, dropping the ruler as he climbed, heard in a clitter-clatter way the rush of an oncoming train, cleft by a sudden frightened, piercing whistle, plunged over the rails, checked for a second or two by the rush of the wind carried by the train, as it went thundering by, saw dimly as in a mist a white-faced driver's mouth opening and shutting frantically; but pulling violently out of the intaking wind of the passing train, he sliddered down the other side of the embankment, ripping his trousers and tearing a rent in his leg with the jagged end of a jutting stone; rushed up the street opposite, turned down the next on the left, pushed open the hall-door of the house, burst into the room, and fell, exhausted and fainting, at his frightened mother's feet.

When he came to himself, his mother was bathing his body with water soothing and warm. The sting in his legs had ceased, for his mother had softened them with vaseline. He stretched his hand out, and gripped his mother's bodice.

'Don't let oul' Hunter or oul' Slogan come near me, Ma,' he pleaded.

'They won't be let within an ace of you,' she answered; 'but why did you come dashing in, and why did they beat you till your poor legs were covered with bunches of weals?'

'Oul' Slogan bet an' bet me because he said I watched an' kep' nix for boys playin' cards behind the buttresses of the church at play-time. I couldn't get out of it for they were biggern me; an' besides, me eyes 'ud be in the way of me seein' how to use me mits in a fight; 'n I didn't want to, but they made me, 'n oul' Slogan came on top of us; 'n because all the boys were biggern me, he bet 'n bet me till he was tired.'

His mother softly fixed the bandage round his bad eye, snuggled him gently under the bed-clothes, bent down and kissed him.

'Rest and sleep sound,' she said, 'and forget all about it till the morning.'

And he lay down safe with her who would watch over him, and wended his way into a deep sleep.

Sean O'Casey *Autobiographies*

Another Beating

'Bunter!' Mr Quelch pointed to the Latin dictionary on his table. 'You placed this book on my door, to fall when I entered my study.'

Billy Bunter jumped. This was quite unexpected. He would not have been surprised to hear something about biscuits missing in Common-Room or bananas from a fifth-form study. But this did surprise him. He goggled at Quelch.

'Do you deny this, Bunter?'

'Oh! Yes, sir! I—I haven't been in this study, sir!' gasped Bunter. 'I—I—I don't know why you should think it was me, sir.'

'Show me your hands, Bunter.'

'Mum-mum-mum-my hands, sir?' stuttered Bunter.

'At once!' rapped Mr Quelch.

Billy Bunter held up two grubby, sticky paws for inspection. Mr Quelch inspected them with a grim eye. Bunter's fat fingers were often sticky. Now they were quite uncommonly sticky. Mauly's jam told its own tale! Billy Bunter's paws were as sticky as Smithy's 'dick'.

'Now, Bunter — !' Quelch's voice was deep.

'It wasn't me, sir!' gasped Bunter. 'I don't know anything about it, sir! I—I haven't touched Smithy's Latin dick, sir—'

'Indeed!' said Mr Quelch, in a grinding voice. 'Then how do you know, Bunter, that this dictionary is Vernon-Smith's?'

'Oh! I—I? I don't know, sir!' groaned Bunter. 'I—I never got it from his study, sir—never thought of it. Never touched it, sir.'

'You have not only touched it, Bunter, but you have left it in a disgustingly sticky state—'

'Oh, crikey!'

'Bunter! You have played a foolish and disrespectful prank in your form-master's study. But that is not all. That, Bunter, is not the most serious aspect of the matter.' Quelch's voice deepened. 'From the name in that book, Bunter, I might have concluded that Vernon-Smith was the offender—I might have punished him in error, Bunter. By borrowing another boy's book to play this foolish prank, Bunter, you might have caused your form-master to commit an act of injustice.'

Billy Bunter goggled at him. Luckily for Bunter, Quelch did not suspect that Smithy's 'dick' had been borrowed for that very purpose!

'That Bunter, is an extremely serious matter—'

'Is – is – is it, sir?' gasped Bunter.

'In such circumstances,' continued Mr Quelch, 'it is my duty to administer a very severe punishment.'

'Oh, lor'!'

Mr Quelch swished that stout cane.

'You will now bend over that chair, Bunter.'

'B-b-b-but I – I say, sir, it wasn't me!' gasped Bunter. 'I – I never touched that dick, sir, and – and I never noticed that I'd made it sticky –'

'Bend over that chair!'

A dismal Owl bent over the chair. From the very bottom of his fat heart, Billy Bunter repented him that he had ever evolved that masterly scheme for killing two birds with one stone! But repentance came too late! The cane was swishing.

Whop! whop! whop!

'Yow-ow-wow!'

Whop! Whop!

'Ow! Ooooooh! Wooooooh!'

WHOP!

It was a full six! And they were laid on well and truly. In such circumstances, as he had said, Quelch felt it his duty to be severe. And Quelch was a whale on duty! Most Remove fellows were aware, from experience, that Quelch could whop! But never before had William George Bunter realized with what energy he could whop! The last swipe elicited a wild yell from the hapless Owl.

'Yarooooooh!'

'Now, Bunter –'

'Wow! wow! Oh, jiminy! Wow!'

'You may leave my study, Bunter.'

'Ow! wow! wow!'

Billy Bunter left it – doubled up like a pocket-knife. Sounds of woe floated back as he crawled down the corridor. Five fellows were waiting for him when he emerged tottering into the quad. But if Harry Wharton and Co. had hostile intentions, they forgot them at the sight of the suffering Owl. In fact his aspect might have melted a heart of stone.

'Hallo, hallo, hallo!' exclaimed Bob Cherry. 'What – ?'

'Ow! Ow! Ooooh! I – I say, you fellows, Quelch knew it was me –

wow! I say, I've had – wooooh! – six! Wow! Ow! Ooooh! Oh, crikey! Did he lay it on! Wow!'

'Ha, ha, ha!'

'Blessed if I see anything to cackle at! I tell you I've had six – wow!'

'Serve you jolly well right!' said Johnny Bull.

'The rightfulness is terrific, my esteemed fat Bunter.'

'Ow! Beast! Wow!'

The fact that, in the opinion of the Famous Five, it served him right, did not seem to comfort Billy Bunter in the very least. It was a sad, suffering, sorrowful Owl. And it was likely to be a long, long, long time, before Billy Bunter evolved any more masterly schemes for killing two birds with one stone!

Frank Richards

Two Dialogues

SON Poor old Mum, mucked it up again.
DAD Don't talk to your mother like that.
MUM Lots of people fail their driving test twice.
DAD Go on, tell us. How many people did you knock down this time?
MUM I didn't . . .
SON Don't know why you bother to try.
DAD Waste of time, if you ask me.
SON And money.
DAD My money.

FRIEND What's that?
HUSBAND Violets for the little woman. Wedding anniversary.
FRIEND Romantic.
HUSBAND Don't know what I'd do without her. Marvellous
 housekeeper. Great mother. Does all my secretarial work too.
FRIEND Do you pay her?
HUSBAND What for? She's my wife. She doesn't need money.

Dinah Brooke

Men and Housework

It seemed perfectly reasonable. We both had careers, both had to work a couple of days a week to earn enough to live on, so why shouldn't we share the housework? So I suggested it to my mate and he agreed – most men are too hip to turn you down flat. 'You're right,' he said. 'It's only fair.'

Then an interesting thing happened. I can only explain it by stating that we women have been brainwashed more than even we can imagine. Probably too many years of seeing television women in ecstasy over their shiny waxed floors or breaking down over their dirty shirt collars. Men have no such conditioning. They recognize the essential fact of housework right from the very beginning. Which is that it stinks. Here's my list of dirty chores: buying groceries, carting them home and putting them away; cooking meals and washing dishes and pots; doing the laundry, digging out the place when things get out of control; washing floors. The list could go on but the sheer necessities are bad enough. All of us have to do these things, or get some one else to do them for us. The longer my husband contemplated these chores, the more repulsed he became, and so proceeded the change from the normally sweet considerate Dr Jekyll into the crafty Mr Hyde who would stop at nothing to avoid the horrors of – *housework*. As he felt himself backed into a corner laden with dirty dishes, brooms, mops and reeking garbage, his front teeth grew longer and pointier, his fingernails haggled and his eyes grew wild. Housework trivial? Not on your life! Just try to share the burden.

So ensued a dialogue that's been going on for several years. Here are some of the high points:

'I don't mind sharing the housework, but I don't do it very well. We should each do the things we're best at.'

Meaning: Unfortunately I'm no good at things like washing dishes or cooking. What I do best is a little light carpentry, changing light bulbs, moving furniture *(how often do you move furniture?)*.

Also Meaning: Historically the lower classes (black men and us) have had hundreds of years experience doing menial jobs. It would be a waste of manpower to train someone else to do them now.

Also Meaning: I don't like the dull stupid boring jobs, so you should do them.

'I don't mind sharing the work, but you'll have to show me how to do it.'

Meaning: I ask a lot of questions and you'll have to show me everything every time I do it because I don't remember so good. Also don't try to sit down and read while I'm doing my jobs because I'm going to annoy hell out of you until it's easier to do them yourself.

'We used to be so happy!' (Said whenever it was his turn to do something.)

Meaning: I used to be so happy.

Meaning: Life without housework is bliss. (*No quarrel here. Perfect agreement.*)

'We have different standards, and why should I have to work to your standards. That's unfair.'

Meaning: If I begin to get bugged by the dirt and crap I will say 'This place sure is a sty' or 'How can anyone live like this?' and wait for your reaction. I know that all women have a sore called 'Guilt over a messy house' or 'Household work is ultimately my responsibility.' I know that men have caused that sore – if anyone visits and the place *is* a sty, they're not going to leave and say, 'He sure is a lousy housekeeper.' You'll take the rap in any case. I can outwait you.

Also Meaning: I can provoke innumerable scenes over the housework issue. Eventually doing all the housework yourself will be less painful to you than trying to get me to do half. Or I'll suggest we get a maid. She will do my share of the work. You will do yours. It's women's work.

'I've got nothing against sharing the housework, but you can't make me do it on your schedule.'

Meaning: Passive resistance. I'll do it when I damned well please, if at all. If my job is doing dishes, it's easier to do them once a week. If taking out laundry, once a month. If washing the floors, once a year. If you don't like it, do it yourself oftener, and then I won't do it at all.

Pat Mainardi

CLEANING WINDOWS
"What a day we're having"

SCRUBBING

TATTING

THE NEW NURSE.

MINDING BABY.

TATTING

THE LAUNDR

NOTHING TO DO

We've got no Work to do-o

FROZEN OUT M. D's

w WE'RE BUSY.

OUR HOUSEMAID

8 O'CLOCK TEA

Life of a Housewife

One of the definitions of automation is a human being acting mechanically in a monotonous routine. Now, as always, the most automated appliance in a household is the mother. Because of the speed at which it's played, her routine has not only a nightmarish but farcical quality to it. Some time ago, the *Ladies' Home Journal* conducted and published a forum on the plight of young mothers. Ashley Montague and some other professionals plus members of the *Journal* staff interviewed four young mothers. Two of them described their morning breakfast routine.

One woman indicated that she made the breakfast, set it out, left the children to eat it, and then ran to the washing machine. She filled that up and ran back to the kitchen, shoved a little food in the baby's mouth, and tried to keep the others eating. Then she ran back to the machine, put the clothes in a wringer, and started the rinse water.

The other woman stated they had bacon every morning so the first thing she does is put the bacon on and the water for coffee. Then she goes back to her room and makes up the bed. 'Generally, I find myself almost running back and forth. I don't usually walk. I run to make the bed.' By that time the pan is hot and she runs back to turn the bacon. She finishes making the children's breakfast and if she is lucky she gets to serve it before she is forced to dash off and attend to the baby, changing him, and sitting him up. She rushes back, plops him in a little canvas chair, serves the children if she has not already done so, and makes her husband's breakfast. And so it goes through the day. As the woman who runs from bed to bacon explains, 'My problem is that sometimes I feel there aren't enough hours in the day. I don't know whether I can get everything done.'

It's like watching an old-time movie in which for technical reasons everyone seems to be moving at three times normal speed. In this case it is not so funny. With the first child it is not as severe.

What hits a new mother the hardest is not so much the increased workload as the lack of sleep. However unhappy she may have been in her childless state, however desperate, she could escape by sleep. She could be refreshed by sleep. And if she wasn't a nurse or airline stewardess she generally slept fairly regular hours in a seven- to nine-hour stretch. But almost all babies returning from the hospital are on something like a four-hour food schedule, and they usually demand some attention in between feedings. Now children differ, some cry more, some cry less, some cry almost all of the time. If you have never, in some period of your life, been awakened and required to function at one in the morning and again at three, then maybe at seven, or some such schedule, you can't imagine the agony of it.

All of a woman's muscles ache and they generally respond with further pain when touched. She is generally cold and unable to get warm. Her reflexes are off. She startles easily, ducks moving shadows, and bumps into stationary objects. Her reading rate takes a precipitous drop. She stutters and stammers, groping for words to express her thoughts, sounding barely coherent – somewhat drunk. She can't bring her mind to focus. She is in a fog. In response to all the aforementioned symptoms she is always close to tears.

What I have described here is the severe case. Some mothers aren't hit as hard, but almost all new mothers suffer these symptoms in some degree and what's more, will continue to suffer them a good part of their lives. The woman who has several children in close succession really gets it. One child wakes the other, it's like a merry-go-round, intensified with each new birth, each childhood illness.

Beverly Jones

When a woman thinks . . . she thinks evil.
Seneca

Nature intended women to be our slaves . . .
they are our property; we are not theirs.
They belong to us,
just as a tree that bears fruit belongs to a gardener.
What a mad idea to demand equality for women! . . .
Women are nothing but machines for producing children.
Napoleon Bonaparte

And a woman is only a woman but a good cigar is a smoke.
Rudyard Kipling

For Him
You have your choice of turntable with
separate tonearm and cartridge of your choice,
or an all-in-one record changer.
The latter also
changes the records automatically.

Let you own ears determine
your choice of speakers. From the variety
made to component high fidelity standards,
you can always find the one you like to listen to.
Music can be piped into other areas of your home
simply by adding speakers.

For Her
This unit plays the record.

The music you hear
comes through the speakers.
They must be kept sufficiently apart.
You need two speakers for stereo.

A woman's place is in the home

Housewives are such dull people

Women's talk is all chatter

If you're so smart why aren't you married

Can you type?

If you want to make decisions in this family,
go out and earn a paycheck yourself

It is a woman's duty to make herself attractive

All women think about are clothes

Women are always playing hard to get

No man likes an easy woman

Women should be struck regularly, like gongs

Women like to be raped

Women are always crying about something

Don't worry your pretty little head about it

Dumb broad

A woman's work is never done

All you do is cook and clean and sit around all day

A woman who can't hold a man isn't much of a woman

Women hate to be with other women

Women are always off chattering with each other

Some of my best friends are women

Woman Is

– kicking strongly in your mother's womb, upon which she is told, 'It must be a boy, if it's so active!'

– being tagged with a *pink* beaded bracelet thirty seconds after you are born, and wrapped in *pink* blankets five minutes thereafter.

– being labelled a tomboy when all you wanted to do was climb that tree and look out and see a distance.

– learning to sit with your legs crossed, even when your feet can't touch the floor yet.

– hating boys – because they're allowed to do things you want to do but are forbidden to – and being told hating boys is a phase.

– wondering why your father gets mad now and then, but your mother mostly sighs a lot.

– seeing grown-ups chuckle when you say you want to be an engineer or doctor when you grow up – learning to say you want to be a mommy or a nurse, instead.

– feeling basically comfortable in your own body, but gradually learning to hate it because you are: too short or tall, too fat or thin, thick-thighed or big-wristed, large-eared or stringy-haired, short-necked or long-armed, bowlegged, knock-kneed or pigeon-toed – *something* that *might* make boys not like you.

– wanting to kill yourself because of pimples, dandruff, or a natural tendency to sweat – and discovering that commercials about miracle products just lie.

– having your first real human talk with your mother and being told about all her old hopes and lost ambitions, and how you can't fight it, and that's just the way it is: life, sex, men, the works – and loving her and hating her for having been so beaten down.

– having your first real human talk with your father and being told about all *his* old hopes and lost ambitions, and how women really have it easier, and 'what a man really wants in a woman,' – and loving him and hating him for having been beaten down – and for beating down your mother in turn.

– coming home from work – and starting *in* to work: unpack the groceries, fix supper, wash up the dishes, rinse out some laundry etc., etc.

– feeling a need to say 'thank you' when your guy actually fixes *himself* a meal now that you're dying with the flu.

Robin Morgan

Mothers and Sons

*(A mining village. MRS GASCOIGNE is the
mother of LUTHER, a collier, married to
MINNIE, and JOE, unmarried.*

*Minnie, angry and disillusioned with Luther,
went off to Manchester without him for a few
days and has just come back to Mrs Gascoigne's
cottage. Luther and Joe have come in. Luther has
said that if Minnie won't look after him then he
might get another woman in – Lizzie Charley.
Joe asks Minnie what she thinks of this.)*

MINNIE He's welcome to Lizzie Charley.

JOE Alright. – She's a nice gel. We'll ax 'er to
come in an' manage th' 'ouse – he can pay 'er.

MINNIE What with?

JOE Niver you mind. Should yer like it?

MINNIE He can do just as he likes.

JOE Then should I fetch her? – should I,
Luther?

LUTHER If ter's a mind.

JOE Should I, then, Minnie?

MINNIE If he wants her.

LUTHER I want somebody ter look after me.

JOE Right tha art. *[Puts his cap on]* I'll say as
Minnie canna look after th' house, will 'er
come. That it?

LUTHER Ah.

MRS GASCOIGNE Dunna be a fool. Tha's had a
can or two.

JOE Well – 'er'll be glad o' the job.

MRS GASCOIGNE You'd better stop him, one of
you.

LUTHER I want somebody ter look after me –
an' tha wunna.

MRS GASCOIGNE Eh dear o' me! Dunna thee be
a fool our Joe.
[Exit Joe]

What wor this job about goin' ter Manchester?

LUTHER She said she wouldna live wi' me, an' so 'er went. I thought 'er'd gone for good.

MINNIE You didn't – you *knew*.

LUTHER I knowed what tha'd towd me – as tha'd live wi' me no longer. Tha's come back o' thy own accord.

MINNIE I never said I shouldn't come back.

LUTHER Tha said as tha wouldna live wi' me. An' tha *didna*, neither, – not for –

MRS GASCOIGNE Well, Minnie, you've brought it on your own head. You put him off, an' you put him off, as if 'e was of no account, an' then all of a sudden you invited him to marry you –

MINNIE Put him off! He didn't need much putting off. He never came any faster than a snail.

MRS GASCOIGNE Twice, to my knowledge, he axed thee – an' what can a man do more?

MINNIE Yes, what! A gramophone in breeches could do as much.

MRS GASCOIGNE Oh, indeed! What ailed him was, he wor in collier's britches, i'stead o' a stool-arsed Jack's.

MINNIE No – what ailed him was that *you* kept him like a kid hanging on to you.

MRS GASCOIGNE An' tha bit thy own nose off, when ter said him nay. For had ter married him at twenty-three, there'd ha' been none of this trouble.

MINNIE And why didn't I? Why didn't I? Because he came in his half-hearted 'I will if you like' fashion, and I despised him, yes I did.

MRS GASCOIGNE And who are *you* to be despising him, I should like to know?

MINNIE I'm a woman, and that's enough. But I know now, it was your fault. You held him, and persuaded him that what he wanted was *you*. You kept him, like a child, you even gave him what money he wanted, like a child. He never roughed it – he never faced out anything. You did all that for him.

MRS GASCOIGNE And what if I did! If you made as good a wife to him as I made a mother, you'd do.

MINNIE Should I? You didn't care what women your sons went with, so long as they didn't love them. What do you care really about this affair of Bertha Purdy? You don't. All you cared about was to keep your sons for yourself. You kept the solid meal, and the orts and slarts any other woman could have. But I tell you, I'm *not* for having the orts and slarts, and your leavings from your sons. I'll have a man, or nothing, I will.

MRS GASCOIGNE It's rare to be some folks, ter pick and choose.

MINNIE I can't pick and choose, no. But what I won't have, I won't have, and that is all.

MRS GASCOIGNE *[to Luther]* Have I ever kept thee from doin' as tha wanted? Have I iver marded and coddled thee?

LUTHER Tha hasna, beguy!

MINNIE No, you haven't, perhaps, not by the look of things. But you've bossed him. You've decided everything for him, really. He's depended on you as much when he was thirty as when he was three. You told him what to do, and he did it.

MRS GASCOIGNE My word, I've never known all he did.

MINNIE You have – everything that mattered. You maybe didn't know it was Bertha Purdy, but you knew it was some woman like her, and what did you care? *She* had the orts and slarts, you kept your son. And you want to keep him, even now. Yes – and you do keep him.

MRS GASCOIGNE We're learnin' a thing or two, Luther.

LUTHER Ay.

[Enter Joe]

MINNIE Yes! What did you care about the woman who would have to take some after you? Nothing! You left her with just the slarts of a man. Yes.

MRS GASCOIGNE Indeed! I canna see as you're so badly off. You've got a husband as doesn't drink, as waits on you hand and foot, as gives you a free hand in everything. It's you as doesn't know when you're well off, madam.

MINNIE I'd rather have had a husband who knocked me about than a husband who was good to me because he belonged to his mother. He doesn't and can't *really* care for me. You stand before him. His *real* caring goes to *you*. Me he only wants sometimes.

JOE She'll be in in a minute.

MRS GASCOIGNE Tha'rt the biggest fool an' jackanapes, our Joe, as iver God made.

MINNIE If she crosses that doorstep, then I go for good.

MRS GASCOIGNE *[bursting into fury – to Joe]* Tha see what thy bobby interferin' has done.

JOE Nay – that's how it stood.

MRS GASCOIGNE Tha mun go an' stop her, our Luther. Tell 'er it wor our Joe's foolery. An' look sharp.

LUTHER What should *I* go for?

[Luther goes out, furious]

MINNIE You see – you see! His mother's word is law to him. He'd do what I told him, but his *feel* would be for you. He's got no *feeling* for me. You keep all that.

MRS GASCOIGNE You talk like a jealous woman.

MINNIE I do! And for that matter, why doesn't Joe marry, either? Because you keep him too. You know, in spite of his bluster, he cares more for your little finger than he does for all the women in the world – or ever will. And it's wrong – it's wrong. How is a woman ever to have a husband, when the men all belong to their mothers? It's wrong.

MRS GASCOIGNE Oh, indeed! – is it? You know, don't you? You know everything.

MINNIE I know this, because I've suffered from it. Your elder sons you let go, and they *are* husbands. But your young sons you've

kept. And Luther is your son, and the man that lives with me.
But first, he's your son. And Joe ought never to marry, for he'd
break a woman's heart.

MRS GASCOIGNE Tha hears, lad! We're bein' told off.

JOE Ah, I hear. An' what's more, it's true, Mother.

MINNIE It is – it is. He only likes playing round me and getting some
pleasure out of teasing me, because he knows I'm safely married
to Luther, and can never look to him to marry me and belong to me.
He's safe, so he likes me. If I were single, he'd be frightened to
death of me.

JOE Happen I should.

MRS GASCOIGNE Th'art a fool.

MINNIE And that's what you've done to me – that's my life spoiled –
spoiled – ay, worse than if I'd had a drunken husband that
knocked me about. For it's dead.

MRS GASCOIGNE Tha'rt shoutin because nowt ails thee – that's
what tha art.

JOE Nay, Mother, tha knows it's right. Tha knows tha's got me –
an'll ha'e me till ter dies – an' after that – yi.

MRS GASCOIGNE Tha talks like a fool.

JOE And sometimes, Mother, I wish I wor dead, I do.

MINNIE You see, you see! You see what you've done to them. It's
strong women like you, who were too much for their husbands –
ah!

JOE Tha knows I couldna leave thee, Mother – tha knows I couldna.
An' me, a young man, belongs to thy owd age. An' there's nowheer
for me to go, Mother. For tha'rt gettin' nearer to death an' yet I
canna leave thee to go my own road. An' I wish, yi, often, as I
wor dead.

MRS GASCOIGNE Dunna, lad – dunna let 'er put these ideas i' thy
head.

JOE An' I can but fritter my days away. There's no goin' forrard
for me.

MRS GASCOIGNE Nay, lad, nay – what lad's better off than thee,
dost reckon?

JOE If I went t'r Australia, th' best part on me wouldna go wi' me.

MRS GASCOIGNE Tha wunna go t'r Australia!

JOE If I went, I should be a husk of a man. I'm allers a husk of a man,
Mother. There's nowt solid about me. The' isna.

MRS GASCOIGNE Whativer dost mean? You've a' set on me at once.

JOE I'm nowt, Mother, an' I count for nowt. Yi, an' I know it.

MRS GASCOIGNE Tha does. Tha sounds as if tha counts for nowt,
as a rule, doesn't ter?

JOE There's not much of a man about me. T'other chaps is more of
fools, but they more of men an' a' – an' they know it.

MRS GASCOIGNE That's thy fault.

JOE Yi – an' will be – ter th' end o' th' chapter.

D. H. Lawrence *The Daughter-in-Law*

A Bit of Rough Handling

(The Pooka, who is a kind of Irish devil, has arrived in Dermot Trellis's bedroom one morning to torment him. He works a powerful piece of magic so that Trellis shoots out of the bedroom window. The Pooka flies out after him.)

The two lads in the air came to a sudden stop by order of his Satanic Majesty. The Pooka himself stopped where he was, never mind how it was done. The other fell down about half a mile to the ground on the top of his snot and broke his two legs in halves and fractured his fourteen ribs, a terrible fall altogether. Down flew the Pooka after a while with a pipe in his mouth and the full of a book of fancy talk out of him as if this was any consolation to our friend, who was pumping blood like a stuck pig and roaring out strings of profanity and dirty foul language, enough to make the sun set before the day was half over.

'Enough of that, my man,' says the Pooka taking the pipe from his mouth. 'Enough of your dirty tongue now, Caesar. Say you like it.'

'I'm having a hell of a time,' says Trellis. 'I'm nearly killed laughing. I never had such a gas since I was a chiseller.'

'That's right,' says the Pooka, 'enjoy yourself. How would you like a kick on the side of the face?'

'Which side?' says Trellis.

'The left side, Caesar,' says the Pooka.

'You're too generous altogether,' says Trellis. 'I don't know you well enough to take a favour like that from you.'

'You're welcome,' says the Pooka. And with these words he walked back, took the pipe out of his jaw, came down with a run and lifted the half of the man's face off his head with one kick and sent it high up into the trees where it got stuck in a blackbird's nest.

'Say you like it,' says he to Trellis quicklike.

'Certainly I like it,' says Trellis through a hole in his head – he had no choice because orders is orders, to quote a well-worn tag. 'Why wouldn't I like it? I think it's grand.'

'We are going to get funnier as we go along,' says the Pooka, frowning with his brows and pulling hard at the old pipe. 'We are going to be very funny after a while. Is that one of your bones there on the grass?'

'Certainly,' says Trellis, 'that's a lump out of my back.'

'Pick it up and carry it in your hand,' says the Pooka, 'we don't want any of the parts lost.'

When he had finished saying that, he put a brown tobacco spit on Trellis's snot.

'Thanks,' says Trellis.

'Maybe you're tired of being a man,' says the Pooka.

'I'm only half a man as it is,' says Trellis. 'Make me into a fine woman and I'll marry you.'

'I'll make you into a rat,' says the Pooka.

And be damned but he was as good as his word. He worked the usual magic with his thumb and changed Trellis by a miracle of magic into a great whore of a buck rat with a black pointed snout and a scaly tail and a dirty rat-coloured coat full of ticks and terrible vermin, to say nothing of millions of plague-germs and disease and epidemics of every description.

'What are you now?' says the Pooka.

'Only a rat,' says the rat, wagging his tail to show he was pleased because he had to and had no choice in the matter. 'A poor rat,' says he. . . .

The Pooka took a good pull at his pipe. The result of this manoeuvre was magic of a very high order, because the Pooka succeeded in changing himself into a wire-haired Airedale terrier, the natural enemy of the rat from the start of time. He gave one bark and away with him like the wind after the mangy rat. Man, but it was a great chase, hither and thither and back again, the pair of them squealing and barking for further orders. The rat, of course, came off second best. He was caught by the throat at the heel of the hunt and got such a shaking that he practically gave himself up for lost. Practically every bone and sinew in his body was gone by the time he found himself dropped again on the grass. . . .

And the short of it is this, that the Pooka worked more magic till himself and Trellis found themselves again in the air in their own bodies, just as they had been a quarter of an hour before that, none the worse for their trying ordeals.

Flann O'Brien *At Swim-Two-Birds*

After the Dentist

My left upper
lip and half

my nose is gone.
I drink my coffee

on the right from
a warped cup

whose left lip dips.
My cigarette's

thick as a finger.
Somebody else's.

I put lip-
stick on a cloth-

stuffed doll's
face that's

surprised when one
side smiles.

May Swenson

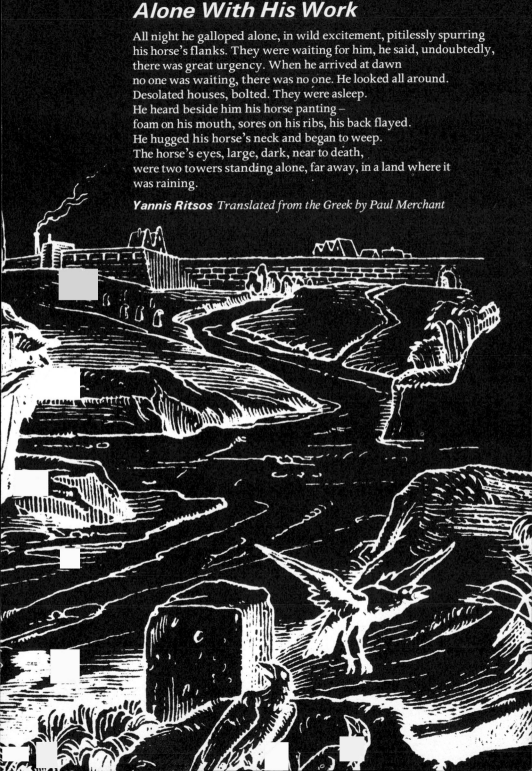

Alone With His Work

All night he galloped alone, in wild excitement, pitilessly spurring
his horse's flanks. They were waiting for him, he said, undoubtedly,
there was great urgency. When he arrived at dawn
no one was waiting, there was no one. He looked all around.
Desolated houses, bolted. They were asleep.
He heard beside him his horse panting –
foam on his mouth, sores on his ribs, his back flayed.
He hugged his horse's neck and began to weep.
The horse's eyes, large, dark, near to death,
were two towers standing alone, far away, in a land where it
was raining.

Yannis Ritsos *Translated from the Greek by Paul Merchant*

Furious Struggle Between Seamen and an Octopus of Colossal Size

The Arrival in Valparaiso

The sailors who came back
from battling with the octopus
have still not taken it in —
they would not travel by train,
they were afraid of the rails,
they lived in fear of suckers
on the rims of rubber tyres,
amongst legs and trees.
They were afraid of the moon!

They lived in gloom, cringing
round taverns and barrels,
their black beards grew
at will, beyond control,
and they behind their beards
were every time more hostile
as if the remote creature
had filled them up with water.

I met them in Valparaiso,
tangled in their hair,
itching, indelicate,
and they seemed offended
not by the great sea monster
but by cigarettes,
by vague conversations,
by glassy-looking drinks.

They read improbable dailies,
Mercurio, Diario Ilustrado,
and sexy magazines
with photographs of goddesses
with fascinating navels,
but they were far away, reading
what will not happen again,
what does not happen twice —
the wars with the cephalopod
which feeds on whaling men,
and since in the daily papers
these things were not reported,
class of fish   they spat in a fury
and shook at such forgetting.

114

The Fight

At sea the sailing boat slept
in the teeth of the night,
the rough sailors snored,
illumined by the moon
and the whale, losing blood,
carried its speared pride
through latitudes of water.

The man awoke to the touch
of eight cold horrors,
eight hosepipes from the deep,
eight tentacles from the silence,
and the proud ship shuddered,
its skyscape tumbled —
a great sea creature gripped it
like a giant hand,
a whole army of suckers
entered the sailors' dream.

The struggle was unbridled
and took on such proportions
that masts snapped off,
axes hacked out pieces
of hard undersea rubber,
the mouths of the monster sucked
through huge layered lips,
while its great lidless eyes
watched through their phosphorescence.

There, it was butchery,
feet slithered in blood,
and when the Beast's cold fingers
fell away, severed,
another grisly arm arose
coiling round the belts
of the luckless Chileans.

When the frozen Antarctic
spread its cloth of dawn —
it found death in the sea —
that sailing boat swept down
by the dying octopus
and seven whalemen alive
between the sea and the silence.

The dawn wept fit to soak
its cloth of yellow water.
Then the birds passed over,
interminable flocks,
hives of the archipelago,
and over the bitter wounds
of the Beast and over the dead
passed the indifferent light
and wings passed over the foam.

The Crew

Roberto Lopez embarked on the *Aurora*.
Arturo Soto in the *Antarctic Star*.
Olegario Ramirez on the *Maipo*.
Justino Pérez died in a brawl.
Sinfín Carrasco is a soldier in Iquique.
Juan de Dios González is a farmer and fells
larch trunks in the   islands of the South.

Pablo Neruda
Translated from the Spanish by Alastair Reid

117

The Crew of the Essex

On 12 August 1819 the *Essex*, a well-found whaler of 238 tons, sailed from Nantucket with George Pollard, Jr as captain, Owen Chase and Matthew Joy mates, six of her complement of twenty men Negroes, bound for the Pacific Ocean, victualled and provided for two years and a half.

A year and three months later, on 20 November 1820, just south of the equator in longitude 119 West, this ship, on a calm day, with the sun at ease, was struck head on twice by a bull whale, a spermeceti about 85 feet long, and with her bows stove in, filled and sank.

Her twenty men set out in three open whaleboats for the coast of South America 2000 miles away. They had bread (200 lb a boat), water (65 gallons), and some Galapagos turtles. Although they were at the time no great distance from Tahiti, they were ignorant of the temper of the natives and feared cannibalism.

Their first extreme sufferings commenced a week later when they made the mistake of eating, in order to make their supply last, some bread which had got soaked by the sea's wash. To alleviate the thirst which followed, they killed turtle for its blood. The sight revolted the stomachs of the men.

In the first weeks of December their lips began to crack and swell, and a glutinous saliva collected in the mouth, intolerable to the taste.

Their bodies commenced to waste away, and possessed so little strength they had to assist each other in performing some of the body's weakest functions. Barnacles collected on the boats' bottoms, and they tore them off for food. A few flying fish struck their sails, fell into the boats, and were swallowed raw.

After a month of the open sea they were gladdened by the sight of a small island which they took to be Ducie but was Elizabeth Isle. Currents and storm had taken them a thousand miles off their course.

They found water on the island after a futile search for it from rocks which they picked at, where moisture was, with their hatchets. It was discovered in a small spring in the sand at the extreme verge of ebbtide. They could gather it only at low water. The rest of the time the sea flowed over the spring to the depth of six feet.

Twenty men could not survive on the island and, to give themselves the chance to reach the mainland before the supplies they had from the ship should be gone, seventeen of them put back to sea 27 December.

The three who stayed, Thomas Chapple of Plymouth, England, and William Wright and Seth Weeks of Barnstable, Mass., took shelter in caves among the rocks. In one they found eight human skeletons, side by side as though they had lain down and died together.

The only food the three had was a sort of blackbird which they caught when at roost in trees and whose blood they sucked. With the meat of the bird, and a few eggs, they chewed a plant tasting like peppergrass which they found in the crevices of the rocks. They survived.

The three boats, with the seventeen men divided among them, moved under the sun across ocean together until 12 January when, during the night, the one under the command of Owen Chase, first mate, became separated from the other two.

Already one of the seventeen had died, Matthew Joy, second mate. He had been buried 10 January. When Charles Shorter, Negro, out of the same boat as Joy, died on 23 January, his body was shared among the men of that boat and the captain's, and eaten. Two days more and Lawson Thomas, Negro, died and was eaten. Again two days and Isaac Shepherd, Negro, died and was eaten. The bodies were roasted to dryness by means of fires kindled on the ballast sand at the bottom of the boats.

Two days later, the twenty-ninth, during the night, the boat which had been Matthew Joy's got separated from the captain's and was never heard of again. When she disappeared three men still lived, William Bond, Negro, Obed Hendricks and Joseph West.

In the captain's boat now alone on the sea, four men kept on. The fifth, Samuel Reed, Negro, had been eaten for strength at his death the day before. Within three days these four men, calculating the miles they had to go, decided to draw two lots, one to choose who should die that the others might live, and one to choose who should kill him. The youngest, Owen Coffin, serving on his first voyage as a cabin boy to learn his family's trade, lost. It became the duty of Charles Ramsdale, also of Nantucket, to shoot him. He did, and he, the captain and Brazilla Ray, Nantucket, ate him.

That was 1 February 1821. On 11 February, Ray died of himself, and was eaten. On 23 February the captain and Ramsdale were picked up by the Nantucket whaleship *Dauphin*, Captain Zimri Coffin.

The men in the third boat, under the command of Owen Chase, the first mate, held out the longest. They had become separated from the other two boats before hunger and thirst had driven any of the *Essex*'s men to extremity. Owen Chase's crew had buried their first death, Richard Peterson, Negro, on 20 January.

It was not until 8 February, when Isaac Cole died in convulsions, that Owen Chase was forced, some two weeks later than in the other boats, to propose to his two men, Benjamin Lawrence and Thomas Nickerson, that they should eat of their own flesh. It happened to them this once, in this way: they separated the limbs from the body, and cut all the flesh from the bones, after which they opened the body, took out the heart, closed the body again, sewed it up as well as they could, and committed it to the sea.

They drank of the heart and ate it. They ate a few pieces of the flesh and hung the rest, cut in thin strips, to dry in the sun. They made a fire, as the captain had, and roasted some to serve them the next day.

The next morning they found that the flesh in the sun had spoiled, had turned green. They made another fire to cook it to prevent its being wholly lost. For five days they lived on it, not using of their remnant of bread.

They recruited their strength on the flesh, eating it in small pieces with salt water. By the fourteenth they were able to make a few attempts at guiding the boat with an oar.

On the fifteenth the flesh was all consumed and they had left the last of their bread, two sea biscuits. Their limbs had swelled during the last two days and now began to pain them excessively. They judged they still had three hundred miles to go.

On the seventeenth the settling of a cloud led Chase to think that land was near. Notwithstanding, the next morning, Nickerson, seventeen years of age, having bailed the boat, lay down, drew a piece of canvas up over him, and said that he then wished to die immediately. On the nineteenth, at seven in the morning, Lawrence saw a sail at seven miles, and the three of them were taken up by the brig *Indian* of London, Captain William Crozier.

It is not known what happened in later years to the three who survived the island. But the four Nantucket men who, with the captain, survived the sea, all became captains themselves. They died old, Nickerson at seventy-seven, Ramsdale, who was nineteen on the *Essex*, at seventy-five, Chase who was twenty-four, at seventy-three, Lawrence who was thirty, at eighty, and Pollard, the captain, who had been thirty-one at the time, lived until 1870, age eighty-one.

The captain, on his return to Nantucket, took charge of the ship *Two Brothers*, another whaler, and five months from home struck a reef to the westward of the Sandwich Islands. The ship was a total loss, and Pollard never went to sea again. At the time of the second wreck he said: 'Now I am utterly ruined. No owner will ever trust me with a whaler again, for all will say I am an unlucky man.' He ended his life as the night watch of Nantucket town, protecting the houses and people in the dark.

Owen Chase was always fortunate. In 1832 the *Charles Carrol* was built for him on Brant Point, Nantucket, and he filled her twice, each time with 2600 barrels of sperm oil. In his last years he took to hiding food in the attic of his house.

Charles Olson *Call Me Ishmael*

John Glashan

... and this is our Children's Model —
Peruvian Mahogany ..

Acknowledgements

Poems and Prose   For permission to use copyright material acknowledgement is made to the following:

For '*A Letter to a Teacher*' by the School of Barbiana to Eda Pelagatti; for 'Prison Comforts' from *The Quare Fellow* by Brendan Behan to Methuen; for 'General, That Tank' and 'Song of the Rice Bargees' by Bertholt Brecht from *Modern German Poetry 1910–1960* edited by Christopher Middleton and Michael Hamburger and translated by Christopher Middleton to MacGibbon & Kee; for 'Two Dialogues' by Dinah Brooke from *Shrew*, vol. 3 to Women's Liberation Workshop; for 'Ain't No Sense in Trying to Take Advantage' from *Manchild in the Promised Land* by Claude Brown to Jonathan Cape; for 'The Deepest Pain' and 'Escape to School' from *Order by View* by René Cutforth to Faber & Faber Ltd; for 'Army Medicine–First World War, Austrian Empire Style' from *The Good Soldier Schweik* by Jaroslav Hašek and translated by Paul Selver to the author and translator; for 'Life of a Housewife' by Beverly Jones from Dynamics of Marriage and Motherhood in *Sisterhood is Powerful*, An Anthology of Writings from the Women's Liberation Movement edited by Robin Morgan to the author; for 'The Arrest' from *The Trial* by Franz Kafka to the author; for 'Taken to a Cell' from *Dialogue with Death* by Arthur Koestler to A. D. Peters & Co; for 'Mothers and Sons' from *The Daughter-in-Law* in *Three Plays* by D. H. Lawrence to Laurence Pollinger Ltd and the Estate of the late Mrs Frieda Lawrence; for 'Bedtime Story', 'Willimantic, Conn.' and 'A Plea to White Men to Join the March on Washington' from *Cold Water* by Lou Lipsitz to Wesleyan University Press; for 'Politics of Housework' by Pat Mainardi from *Sisterhood is Powerful*, An Anthology of Writings from the Women's Liberation Movement edited by Robin Morgan to the author; for 'Woman Is' by Robin Morgan from *Sisterhood is Powerful*, An Anthology of Writings from the Women's Liberation Movement edited by Robin Morgan to the author; for 'The Pueblo' and 'Furious Struggle Between Seamen and an Octopus of Colossal Size' by Pablo Neruda from *Selected Poems* edited by Nathaniel Tarn and translated by Robert Bly and Alastair Reid to Jonathan Cape; for 'A Bit of Rough Handling by the Devil' from *At Swim-Two-Birds* by Flann O'Brien to MacGibbon & Kee; for 'Johnny Casside, Receiving his First Pay Packet, Discovers that he has been Fined Two Shillings out of Seven and Six for "Impudence and Disobedience"' and 'A Beating' from *Autobiographies* by Sean O'Casey to the Macmillan Co. of London and Basingstoke; for 'The Hangman' by Maurice Ogden (words from a film of the same name) to the author; for 'The Crew of the Essex' from *Call Me Ishmael* by Charles Olson to Jonathan Cape and the Estate of Charles Olson; for 'Another Beating' from *Alas Poor Bunter* by Frank Richards to the Hamlyn Publishing Group Limited; for 'Alone With His Work' by Yannis Ritsos translated by Paul Merchant to the author and the translator; for 'After the Dentist' from *Half Sun, Half Sleep* by May Swenson to the author and Charles Scribner's Sons; for 'The Destruction of the Red Indian' by Alexis de Tocqueville from *Democracy in America* edited by J. P. Mayer to Harper & Row Inc.; for 'P.O.W.' from *Slaughterhouse Five* by Kurt Vonnegut to the author and Jonathan Cape; for 'Hamp is Questioned about Desertion by his Defending Officer, Desertion Carrying the Death Penalty' by John Wilson to Curtis Brown Ltd; for 'Sentence' from *A Life* by Zeno to the Macmillan Co. of London and Basingstoke.

Pictures   For the pictures on pages 8–9 to Camera Press; pages 10–11 to Radio Times Hulton
Picture Library; pages 12–13 to the Victoria and Albert Museum; pages 14–15 to
Rogner & Bernhardt Publishers; pages 16–17 to The Publicity Bureau of
Gelsenkirchen, Germany; page 20 to John Freeman; page 22 to The Museum of
Modern Art; pages 26–7 to The John Hillelson Agency; pages 28–9 to Camera Press;
pages 34–5 to Harry N. Abrams Inc. Publishers, New York; pages 36–7 to Andrew
de Lory; pages 38–9 to Dover Publications Inc.; pages 44–5 to Snark International;
page 47 to Snark International; page 48 to The Philadelphia Museum of Art Collection;
pages 52–3 to The Byron Collection Museum, Museum of City of New York;
pages 60–61 to Janine Wiedel; pages 66–7 to The Museum of Modern Art, New York;
page 68 to the University of Nebraska Press; page 70 to The Thomas Gilcrease
Institute; pages 72–3 to Di Frighi Fulvio; pages 74–5 to The Portal Gallery; page 87 to
Larry Herman; pages 89, 91 from the *Magnet*, published by Howard Baker Publishers;
pages 95, 100, 101 from *Le Masque*, by Saul Steinberg published by Maeght Editeur;
page 99 to The Collection Tom Benenson, New York; page 102 to the National
Museum, Stockholm; page 104 to Ben Shahn and The Museum of Modern Art, New
York; page 109 to David Hockney and The Petersberg Press; page 111 to the Klee
Foundation; pages 114–15 to Ardea Photographics; pages 116–17 to The Bettmann
Archives; page 118 to The Radio Times Hulton Picture Library and the Victoria and
Albert Museum; page 122 to John Glashan.

Every effort has been made to trace owners of copyright material, but in some cases
this has not proved possible. The publishers would be glad to hear from any further
copyright owners of material reproduced in *The Receiving End*.

List of Illustrations

Index